The Clare Young Environmentalists
(alias Clare Youth Impact)

A social, educational and environmental exercise

By

Hugh W. L. Weir

BALLINAKELLA PRESS
1998

© 1998 Hugh W. L. Weir
Ballinakella Press
Whitegate, Co. Clare, Ireland

First Published 1998

ISBN 0 946538 22 0

Editing: Anna-Maria Hajba
Book Design: Hugh W. L. Weir
Typesetting: Anna-Maria Hajba and Grania R. Weir
Cover: Northern and Southern Environmentalists

Preface and Acknowledgements

Since the 1996 Christmas CYE-reunion, members, friends and parents have expressed interest in a record of our activities. Compiling an autobiographical chapter from scant resourses, I siezed the opportunity to extend my research. The result is neither complete nor absolutely accurate; therefore, I ask my readers' forbearance. Any inaccuracies or omissions are entirely unintentional. These pages are compiled in good faith to record the activities of wonderful people who have done so much to promote what was, at the beginning of the 1980s, a new concept of environmental concern and action. They have played a positive rôle for the future of Ireland; their influence extends even further.

I thankfully acknowledge the advice and assistance of George and Maura Hitching who mooted the idea, Brendan Ringrose for filling many gaps with his recollections, Ray Conway for his reading of the final draft, my wife Grania for her support and efforts, Minister Síle de Valera and many others who have smoothed my path. Thank you, too, members and supporters without whom this record could not have been written.

I also thankfully acknowledge the financial contributions of Michael Houlihan of Ennis, Bell'acards, and Brendan Ringrose. Their generosity has helped towards making this little book a worthy keepsake and heirloom, not only for CYE members but for the wider community.

Hugh W. L. Weir, D. Litt.

Clare Young Environmentalists

A social, educational and environmental exercise

DEDICATION

This little book is dedicated
to all those members, supporters and friends
who helped the Clare Young Environmentalists to be
a useful and succesful organisation for
the promotion of environmental
concern and action

FOREWORD
by Síle de Valera

I am happy to write a foreword for Dr. Weir's book in *The Clare Young Environmentalists* (alias Clare Youth Impact). Here, we have set down what I might call a loose diary chronicling the ups and downs, the growth, and at times, the stagnation of an idea and an ideal that was given a reality in the Clare Young Environmentalists.

Dr. Weir, in his preface, describes the book as a keepsake and heirloom. As Minister with responsibility for our heritage, I would describe it as setting down part of our recent folklore. It is part of our written heritage and for much of its content describes an era that has so quickly gone. We can admire the idealism that led to the founding of the Clare Young Environmentalists almost 20 years ago. We can enjoy and, at times, laugh at the various high points and be sad at the misfortunes that are set down in the book – the spread of the ideals of the group, the visit of President Hillery in 1984, the ecumenical and cross cultural activities that embraced both sides of the border and so on. On the sad side, the less said about the hotel in London and the Summer camp of 1988 the better.

To say more would spoil the book for the reader. I would like to commend Dr. Weir for his work in the important area of our environment over the years of hope that those who read this little book will derive pleasure from it and will appreciate what was achieved particularly in the early days, a time when concern for the future of our environment was not perhaps as high on the agenda as it should have been.

SÍLE DE VALERA, T.D.
MINISTER FOR ARTS, HERITAGE,
GAELTACHT AND THE ISLANDS

CHAPTER ONE

Thanks to a father who was interested in nature, and a generally environmentally orientated family, I have always taken an interest in the many facets which influence our lives. As a countryman too, I have been lucky to have been brought up with the simplicity of rural life. I also have an enquiring mind and have always been happy to share my experiences and the little knowledge I have gained, especially with young people.

One of my most satisfying occupations has been self-imposed, or rather born of frustration. During the first six years of married life, my wife Grania and I continued an involvement with *An Taisce*, the National Trust for Ireland; unlike other trusts, it embraced most elements of the environment. As the only prescribed Irish environmental organization with any clout, its voluntary membership did a good job. We were both members of the Clare Committee. Many co-members felt, however, that more could be done to encourage youth to become involved in environmental work, even concern. We also felt that the national organization was concentrating on Dublin at the expense of rural Ireland; the destruction of Georgian street-scenes or the protection of magpies in St. Stephen's Green could receive much more sympathetic support than, say, stopping the destruction of a primaeval forest in the west. I resigned, after unsuccessfully attempting to promote my suggestions. I received no response from headquarters, even though I had elucidated full reasons for my action; I had hoped that the National Council might have been more positive, if only to question why.

A number of friends expressed support. Several indicated that a group concerned with the Clare environment should be formed to encourage youth; I should give the lead. At 7.30 pm on Friday, 11th April, 1980, I chaired an open meeting in the diningroom extension of the Old Ground Hotel in Ennis. The management of the hotel had always been friendly and accommodating; for many years hence, it was to provide free accommodation for our meetings and events.

About forty young people came, mainly through word of mouth. I had asked for no adult representation; I didn't wish to intrude on Clare *An Taisce*. I knew only a small percentage of these children and youths, mainly through their parents; the rest were total strangers.

1

My efforts to promote environmental awareness through my recently established weekly column in the local newspaper, the *Clare Champion,* were recognised.

Such enthusiasm was displayed by those present that, rather than ascertain whether it would be feasible to found a youth organization, we would grasp the nettle. An excellent debate produced some sensible suggestions. Anxious that the organization be seen to be democratically run by the young members themselves, I arranged for an immediate election. Most present offered themselves as candidates, there being few who didn't know the others, two or three were from Miltown Malbay, others from East Clare, but the greatest number came from Ennis.

A committee of twelve was formed under the chairmanship of Neil Dargan, son of the *Clare Champion* accountant. I knew Neil to be serious and responsible, with very supportive parents. In fact, the parents of the founder members were outstanding in their generosity and support. Any time that transport was needed, they turned up with their cars; equipment was never wanting, and the odd few pounds were pressed into our hands.

It was decided that *The Clare Young Environmentalists* would consist of 10 to 18 year-old children irrespective of creed, sex or race. The membership fee would be £1 per annum so that nobody who wished to join should be excluded. The organization would, where possible, be run by its members with adults merely acting in an advisory capacity. I was asked to be the first President, and Sister Francis O'Dwyer, a teacher in Colaiste Mhuire - the large Ennis girls' secondary school - was to be elected Vice President. The Roman Catholic and Church of Ireland Bishops of Killaloe were asked to be patrons. Bishops Michael Harty, Edwin Owen and their successors were always supportive. The aims of CYE would be the promotion of environmental concern and action by the members amongst the young and adult population. Recognition of the environment was something new. Many times we were asked as to what exactly the word meant; my answer was that the environment concerned was all-embracing: we would not be merely a group of single-issue fanatics. Everything which influenced our lives was part of our brief. Everybody, especially Christians of all denominations, had a moral responsibility to work together for the good of all. If we were to pull together, we had to have an ecumenic and apolitical ethos. This was maintained throughout our active existence. We also supported an all-Ireland approach to environmental problems; this would mean cross-border co-operation.

During the first year, committee meetings were held almost once a month. The first major activity organized was a clean-up of a stretch of the River Fergus near Ballyalla. In poor weather, more than twenty members and almost as many parents turned up to remove old bedsteads, broken bottles and general rubbish. A party from the Ennis branch of the *Society for the Prevention of Cruelty to Animals* also helped, and a nearby hardware company provided a truck to transport what had been collected to the dump. There was also a visit to Craggaunowen where participants toured the crannog, ring fort and Tim Severnin's leather boat, the *St. Brendan*. In August, Ballinakella Lodge was the venue for a general meeting and a discussion on future activities, followed by a boat trip to Iniscealtra (Holy Island) and a talk by our Ennis-based friend and supporter Gerry O'Connell. Gerry, a delightfully modest but well-read local historian, was able to communicate with young people.

The end of September saw quite a crowd cleaning up Spanish Point beach on the Atlantic Coast. Local people, young and old, assisted in the scavenging of some thirty sackfuls of rubbish. *Miltown Malbay Development Association,* through their Honorary Secretary, Michael Fitzpatrick, thanked the participants most sincerely for their work: *"Should you decide to engage in such an effort in our area again, we would be grateful for an opportunity of discussing with you in advance what co-operation we could offer you and what contribution we could make."* It was great to receive his encouraging letter.

Nature Photographer David Hely Hutchinson, married to Grania's cousin, the artist Geraldine O'Brien, gave an informative illustrated talk on wildlife and wildlife photography in October. We had soon realized that there were several streams of interest amongst members: those who were interested in wildlife came to wildlife events but seldom to clean-ups, and vice versa. After David's talk, the interest in photography increased, and members asked sensible questions about their recently acquired cameras. Following the success of the October talk, Mount Callan in West Clare was chosen for a CYE visit on the afternoon of Saturday, 15th November. Unaccompanied children as well as those with their families listened attentively as Robert Tottenham showed us his demesne and forest on the south face of the mountain. Our final event for 1980, our first year, was a pre-Christmas party in the Mary Assumpta Hall in Ennis.

After nine months working and playing together, the membership of CYE had jelled; activities were being enjoyed by the participants. There was enthusiasm and we were thrilled that the organization had got off to a successful start.

Members produced a three-sheet newsletter, *Clare Young Environmentalists*. Most of the first page was taken up by a letter from the founder but Deirdre Cosgrove drew a fox, there was a crossword, and a letter to the editor from Carol McMahon about a recently freed, but once weed-choked river. In his editorial, Chairman Neil Dargan today a priest serving St. Flannan's College in Ennis, said: *"We want to generate a community spirit and an awareness about the environment and the dangers threatening it from pollution, toxic waste, etc."* Ciara McMahon also wrote a chamming piece on winter walks. This newsletter was the first of an increasingly professional annual production of journals and magazines. Members were encouraged to express themselves by writing and by public speaking; many have since become media professionals.

CYE was the only environmental organization in Ireland for ten to eighteen year olds, and membership of a national youth body was now necessary to provide insurance at a reasonable rate. I undertook much of the publicity and arranged for our friends to give talks or demonstrations. The local young people who had joined, together with a few American, English, Italian and other nationalities, were delightfully open and unambiguous; each helped the other. Adults entered into the spirit of the organization. Parents generously provided transport and food, and friends were drawn in to talk or supervise.

Our only income was the annual subscription paid by each member; soon we realized that more was needed and organized flag days, draws and competitions. The *Clare Vocational Education Committee* also generously helped us. The annual magazines paid for themselves. We were insistant that where possible, members should raise their own funds; when there was active fundraising, each would more appreciate their responsibilities.

CHAPTER TWO

In January 1981, there was another gathering at Ballyalla. A popular Ennis place of recreation, the lake and its adjoining area attracted litter. Bags of rubbish were collected before the party moved on to the near-by Templemaley Abbey and adjoining woodland to discuss and help alleviate the problems of ivy. Quite a few trees were freed of their encumbrances.

Neil Dargan's elected committee now considered it important that the general membership had a greater say in the organization, so after each meeting, anyone who had something to contribute would be invited to participate in further discussion. A Killaloe to Scariff Road clean-up was suggested and, on Saturday March 14th, five car-loads of members filled two trailers-full with an assortment of plastic, bottles and papers. The following week there was a better turnout when the ancient Corrovorrin graveyard near Ennis, now surrounded by housing, was given a thorough tidying. Not only was rubbish removed, but some of the participants learnt about their ancestors through tombstone inscriptions; they were also taught how to rub a handful of grass over the letters in order to read them, useful for later visits to other similar sites. A record of these headstones was later presented to Gerry O'Connell for the benefit of the *Clare Archaeological and Historical Society.*

The 1981 Annual General Meeting was held at the Old Ground Hotel in April. It had been decided that as there seemed to be little encouragement for people in general to involve themselves in their environment, a number of awards would be presented each year. Four Ennis businessmen and Leslie Atkins of McKenzies of Cork, all friends or business associates, agreed to sponsor shields. Maurers, the O'Connell Street jewellers, gave the environmental Education Award, and travel agent Tom Mannion looked after that for Industry. The Galvins and Frank O'Dea of the *Clare Champion* were responsible for donating the award for Wildlife Protection and the Director of the West County Inn for that of Self-Giving. Leslie's gift was dedicated to the field of History. The first awardees were Mary Angela Keane for her lectures and talks on the Burren *(Education),* Rick Bolens of the *Institute for Industrial Research and Standards* for his free-time environmental work *(Nature),* Joe Murphy of Scariff for fighting pollution and organizing the re-stocking of the Shannon *(Self-Giving)*, Richard Oldfield of the Old Ground Hotel *(Industry)*, and historian Gerry O'Connell *(History)*.

The second CYE publication, known as the *Trident*, was also distributed in 1981. A more professional production than the first, it had an article on the awards ceremony by Neil Dargan and an evocative photograph of the 1980 Ballyalla clean-up on its front page. The Cosgrove sisters wrote on pine martins, Tina Normile on the World's Biggest Flower, Margaret O'Sullivan about Spring Walks and Caron McMahon on Birds of All Seasons. Shells and Seaweed and articles of general interest, together with a crossword and jokes, added further interest. *Trident* sponsors included Weirs of Whitegate, Sparlings of Scariff, Michael McMahon & Son of Ennis, and Douglas C. Fonda, Jr. of Mountshannon, all of whose financial contributions were thankfully acknowledged.

In May, there was a visit to the Burren; this included the valley of Clab, some spectacular natural caves and various sites near the village of Carron. Participants brought their own food and parents provided transport. A general meeting took place in Ennis in June. The following month, a crowd gathered to clear the neglected St. Joseph's well off the Gort road, north of Ennis; a thorough job was done and, apart from scrub removal, statues were cleaned and painted, and walls restored. Later, there was a small ceremony to celebrate the re-opening and re-dedication of this place of pilgrimage; expressions of appreciation were extended to those who had participated. The following Saturday, Gerry O'Connell conducted a successful historical tour to Corofin; photographs were taken of Thomas Gleeson, Kieran Roughan and other members precariously perched on the walls of de Clare's Kitchen, a medieval fort at Kilnaboy.

Another clearing session was undertaken in Drumcliffe cemetery in August but the task was far too great for the numbers participating; they did their best to remove briars and overgrowth from awkward terrain encumbered with treacherous holes and fallen tombstones. It was felt that another attempt should be made in September.

Brendan O'Regan, hotelier and founder of the Shannon Free Airport concept, had by now formed *Co-Operation North*, a hands across the Irish political border organization with significant voluntary representation from both sides. In November, Executive of the group

John J. Walsh wrote thanking me for information on CYE and for the suggestion for an interchange of young citizens from the Mid-West with those from some areas in the North. He said that he had mentioned CYE as *"providing a valuable example of meaningful activity for the young"* in lectures he had delivered in Belfast's St. Anne's Cathedral and in the Servite Monastery in Benburb. He ended his letter: *"We intend to pursue your suggestion actively in the near future and we will certainly be glad to avail of your kind offer to help"*.

I had written to him suggesting that as there was a shared interest, free from politics or religious denominationalism, a useful exercise would be to bring environmentally aware children together from either side of the border. In the original official draft of the project John Walsh wrote: *"The programme would be under the control of a Director. It would be a good augury for its success that the founder of the Young Environmentalists, Mr. Hugh Weir, has agreed to accept the post on a part time basis"*. His estimated annual costs, for submission to the European Community for grant-aid came to about £35,000. I felt that I already had plenty of work in hand. However, CYE was to gain considerably from exchanges with young people from County Fermanagh, which for the Northern participants were partly financed from the programme's funds.

Other activities included a well-attended talk on eels by our friend, author and *Department of the Marine* fisheries expert Dr. Christopher Moriarty, a summer neighbour at Whitegate; there was girl-scream as he displayed a wriggling slimy creature. A seminar on clans and how to find out about ancestors and their connection with localities at Ballinakella Lodge on a November Saturday had a small but dedicated attendance. At the beginning of December, a speaker from the *Electricity Supply Board* contributed to an evening discussion on nuclear energy, which drew a heated response.

Although there were one or two more events during 1981, I had too little time to supervise CYE activities and Sister Francis, Dick Cronin and other adults were fully involved in teaching. It was a cold winter, road conditions were not conducive to the undertaking of trips to Ennis, and Grania and I were feeling a financial pinch.

CHAPTER THREE

Although there were committee meetings in January 1982, little practical work was done until a general gathering on the 13th of February, when a thorough job was done at the small park between the River Fergus and the Maid of Erin on the outskirts of Ennis. With the co-ordination of the *Urban District Council*, weeds were eliminated and rubbish collected. Most of a long metal railing and the haven's entrance gates were painted. While the work was being undertaken, pedestrians shouted encouragement from the Mill Bridge above; mixed comments were returned as to how they also could share the work. For several years, the area looked really healthy and the local population showed a respect not previously evident.

I was away again for much of March, so although the committee met, there were no activities. I insisted that there had to be adult supervision where there was any likelihood of injury; I was responsible, insurance certificates being in my name. It is so easy for a child to slip and break a leg or, worse, to receive a friendly nudge beside a river, slip and drown. Luckily, although we did have a number of minor accidents, I had little fear of paedophilia or child abuse; the community from which these children were drawn was pretty close and neighbourly. I was as open as I felt justifiable in my answers to often awkward questions; I sympathise with those in the teaching, youth organization or social service spheres today. Young people have a natural interpretation of life, which needs positive confirmation and sympathetic understanding.

During this second year of the eighties, I visited Newbridge College in County Kildare by request of Fr. O'Beirne whom I had met several times with our friend Harriet Waldron in Galway; he was impressed by our organization. A school group was formed under the active chairmanship of pupil Shane Andrews, who was later succeeded by Bernard O'Sullivan and Joseph Dargan. Another priest at the school, Fr. Brennan, was generous in his support, as also was Fr. Mac-Cionaoith. Committee members Colm Webb, Jim O'Connell and Roger Price of County Kildare were amongst those who worked hard to ensure the branch's success. There were about 35 active members.

Other groups were soon set up at Athgarvan (by Adrianne Whyte) and Clane, mainly involving local primary schools, one of whose teachers was from Clare. They mainly involved themselves in clean-ups. Subsequently the *Young Environmentalist Federation* was founded. Due to expense and lack of time to organize on my part, there were only a few associated groups. Apart from Clare, there were two in Dublin and others in Cavan, Mayo and Wicklow. There was considerable interest from other localities, including Belfast, Dungannon and Cork.

The 1982 Annual General Meeting took place on Sunday, 18th April. County Council Chairman Tadhg Macconmara spoke encouragingly that his Council was extremely interested in the work of CYE in such fields, which took physical and moral courage; young people were giving an example to their peers. He then presented the annual awards, a further three being added to those of 1981. Dan Liddy, a national teacher from Cratloe, who had encouraged his pupils to produce a comprehensive local history, was recognized for his efforts in the field of Education; he was introduced by Deirdre O'Callaghan. Thomas McMahon introduced Brian Mooney of the Burren Perfumery, recipient of the Tom Mannion Shield for Industry. Artist Hillary Gilmore, Robert Tottenham, Sister Francis O'Dwyer, Brendan O'Donoghue of Ballyvaughan and ex-Chairman Neil Dargan were also recognized for their achievements in their respective fields. Ray Conway, nowadays involved in film-making, relinquished his Chairmanship to Neil Dargan for the latter's second term. Ray was highly commended, especially for his wording and compilation of the organization's constitution, which was adopted by the membership. Caron McMahon became Secretary, Deirdre Kelly, now an air hostess, was elected Membership Secretary, Ray Conway Public Relations Officer, and Christy O'Donovan, Fiona Cosgrove and Aine Keane were amongst the new committee members.

Other events during the year included a fascinating walk of the Doolin area by County Clare author and historian Sean Spellissy. He showed participants many of the smaller monuments, which are seldom mapped, as well as a number of ring forts and earthworks. Also in June, about twenty members undertook a cycle ride visiting castles, dolmens and church ruins west of Ennis. Kieran Roughan showed us an interesting cave. I was extremely nervous for the safety of the participants and followed in my car; the narrow and twisty Lahinch road was particularly daunting. I indicated my displeasure when those who arrived at Shalee before me had already climbed the dangerous castle walls.

The most significant outing of the year was our first bus tour to County Fermanagh. For £17 each, members left Ennis early on Saturday, 31st July, accompanied by Sister Francis and me. We had hired a Limerick-based bus and stopped at Roscommon Castle for a break. Here participants excitedly clambered over the walls and through the turrets of the vast Anglo-Norman fortification and photographs were taken. There was another stop at Carrick on Shannon where we considered the course of Ireland's longest river, which also borders Clare. After a sandwich lunch on the lawn of Florencecourt House, a National Trust property near Enniskillen, participants were shown round the house by Mr. Paterson-Morgan, their local manager. Some of the children examined the original Florencecourt Yew in the well-maintained gardens.

Thanks to my friends and relations such as the Loanes and Margaret Sides, Clare-connected Rachel Burrows' daughter, we were greeted by Deputy Mayor Cecil Noble on behalf of Enniskillen, the Fermanagh capital. Helen Hickey, Kilkenny-born curator, showed us over the Civic and Military Museums though they were officially closed to the public. I tried to discourage members from convenience foods but little else was available at a reasonable price. After a rapid meal, we boarded Mr. Wilson's *Golden Arrow*, a sixty-five seater water-bus, which took us on a guided tour of Lough Erne, including Devenish Island. On our return it poured with rain, which continued throughout the night. This made little difference to everyone's comfort, however, for we were exhausted by the time our heads were laid to rest, at the Church Hill Hostel near Derrygonnelly.

The rain had cleared somewhat by the following morning, when each attended services in their respective churches. Roman Catholic Mass finished earlier than the Church of Ireland service, so the congregation at the latter was surprised and moved when joined by a crowd of Roman Catholic children who poured into their pews led by a nun in full habit; it had never happened before. After church, participants were greeted by the retired Church of Ireland Bishop of Clogher,

Dr. Heavener, who had conducted the service; his family had originated in County Limerick. The Lord Lieutenant of County Fermanagh, the late Dowager Duchess of Westminster, also greeted and welcomed the party; many expressed surprise that we knew each other, Fermanagh seeming so far from Clare.

Warren Loane then gave a talk at Monea Castle after which Dick and Joan Brandon invited everyone for coffee at their home, Castletown. At the Lough Navar lookout in the mountains above Lower Lough Erne, Warren and I pointed to distant County Donegal and the Atlantic; sadly, it was hazy and overcast.

The driver of the bus, a Limerick-based teacher, indicated that he had to get the vehicle home early as he had another appointment. I told him that we had booked and paid for two whole days and insisted that he drive us to Marble Arch caves. Unfortunately we were too late to visit the tourist centre but the most energetic of us walked the riverside path up to the natural feature, which gives the cave its name. It hadn't changed since my youth when it was one of my excursions from Portora, my old boarding school at Enniskillen. I enjoyed sharing one of my favourite haunts with young people from another part of Ireland, which I also loved, and who would otherwise probably never have ventured over the Border. Parents, too, were wonderfully supportive. The party included Neil's father, Bill Dargan, and a couple of neighbours from Whitegate and Mountshannon.

Twenty-two children and six adults joined us for lunch at Ballinakella Lodge on 14th August. This was followed by a boat trip to Hare Island. It poured with rain, so we returned earlier than expected. The cups of tea and other refreshments were welcomed enthusiastically.

CHAPTER FOUR

As Ireland's first and only environmental organization totally dedicated to young people, CYE had gained an excellent reputation. By 1983, it had over a hundred members, and young people from other parts of Ireland were asking for help. There was a new awareness of the environment. Unfortunately, few adults were prepared to undertake responsibilities and I couldn't be in more than one place at a time; my prime responsibility was to Clare. The government, however, was beginning to recognize the environment as a vote catcher; the Department of Education was also taking a more constructive interest. There were calls for positive action from teachers, County Councils, environmental bodies, many of them recently founded, and the increasing number of Tidy Towns Committees and community councils.

The first major event of 1983 was an evocative talk by Cork-woman and scientist Dr. Irene Daly on recycling. She joined us over a meal at Whitegate before we drove to Ennis for her lecture; she had a fascinating command of her study. The usual committee meetings in January and February were held in the Galvins' Ennis house; the family were always generous in their support. Anthony Galvin was now in the Chair; an individualist, his term was characterful.

In the spring, the Annual General Meeting in the Old Ground Hotel preceded the presentation of Awards. Fiona Cosgrove was elected to succeed Anthony Galvin to the Chair, Deirdre Kelly became the Vice-Chairperson, Caron McMahon's Secretaryship was taken on by Maeve Houlihan, assisted by Jennifer Dinan, and Deirdre O'Callaghan became Treasurer.

Rita Childers presented the Awards. It was the first time she had stayed at Ballinakella since 1973, when Erskine (then President of Ireland) and she spent the night for opening Whitegate's Teach na Féile. A large crowd of public representatives, parents and CYE members supported the presentation.

Shannon Development was recognized with the Industry Award for its Ballycasey Craftshops. The CYE Member's Award was given to P.J. Kenny while Phil Brennan of Shannon was presented with the *Clare Champion's* Wildlife Shield. Solicitor Michael Houlihan, Maeve's father, got the Old Ground Award for Architecture and Design for the then newly-developed Abbey Arcade in Ennis. The

Very Reverend Maurice Talbot, an old friend and supporter, accepted the West County Inn Shield for giving the nation his collection of farm machinery at Bunratty Folk Park. Ignatius Cleary, founder of the Clare Heritage Centre at Corofin, and Risteárd Ua Cróinín of the Ennis Boys National School and restorer of Dysert O'Dea Castle, received recognition regarding History and Genealogy, and Environmental Education, respectively.

Mrs. Childers, in her preliminary speech recalled that *"Clare would always be remembered as the pioneers of this organization, founded in 1980, which is now nationwide. President Childers said on many platforms that this is the finest little country on God's living earth and we must fight to keep it so. Fifty-one percent of the nation was under 25 years of age and what they were doing and thinking during their leisure hours, so lies the whole future of the nation . . . "*

After the award ceremony, Pat Costelloe, the Shannon-based local historian, gave a slide presentation on the history of Clare, assisted by John O'Brien and Sean Spellissy. Bishop Michael Harty and Deputy Sylvester Barrett, who was to become the State's first Minister for the Environment, were amongst those present. A group from Newbridge had come by mini-bus; we shared a trip to the Burren the following day. A photograph of Shannon Development's W.B. Moloney, Lucy Erridge representing the Craftworkers, Rita Childers and me appeared in the *Clare Champion* when Gerry Collison, later to become editor, wrote the event up in *About Shannon*. The previous week, there had been a picture of Ray Conway and Maurice Talbot.

Three days after the 1983 presentations, I visited Athgarvan National School on the Curragh where student Niall O'Keeffe had asked for help to establish their local association. In May we had a tour of the Fenloe District of County Clare and another clean-up at Spanish Point, where a lot of rubbish had got caught up at the mouth of the local river. We had a street tour of Ennis, another Doolin trip, and a fascinating tour of Inchicronan by local historian and author, Tom Coffey, in June.

July saw the first of our annual summer camps. These, like the organization itself, were non-profit ventures. Most of the participants were already CYE members, others had read about the events in my *Clare Champion* column. The weekly newspaper was a most useful publicity vehicle and editor Frank O'Dea generous in his support. The charge of £30 went towards the cost of insurance, food and tours. A tent 'village' was set up in the field beside our garden; this gave access to the lakeshore, but was just far enough to be independent of the house and to allow Grania and me a degree of privacy. Our outside toilet facilities were available, and a lot of wet-weather cooking was done under shelter in our upper yard, usually in a garage.

Each year we would play Kim's game to encourage participants to be observant. A trayful of miscellaneous items would be displayed for some minute or so, then withdrawn. Pens and papers were then issued so that participants would list those remembered. Those who recalled the most received a prize. Another popular tradition was the tasting of wild foods such as dandelions, sorrel, nettles and eels; there was a lot of squeamishness amongst the girls when the latter were presented. Campers were expected to undertake their share of cooking and cleaning-up. Each morning, and at other times, there was a swim; this meant that even in the most inclement weather, I had to don my togs for fear of difficulties. There were lakeshore and mountain walks, night patrols, visits to such establishments as the Portumna Wildlife Park or Craggaunowen and, each day, free time for individuals to join with others for trips to the village or to their local friends. Craftspeople, like Allie Kay, who taught them basic weaving, or Vivienne Foley, pottery, were most generous with their time. There was a lot of good fun, though there were some headaches, such as when items of personal property were mislaid. There were some injuries, although nothing serious; there was also the usual problem of mixed ages and mixed sexes in close-quartered tents. Many times in all weathers I had to leave my comfortable bed, dress and make my way over to the camp to bellow "*shut up*" or "*if I hear another sound...*" They were great kids and, on the whole, well behaved.

The eighteen 1983 participants included Jennifer Dinan, P.J. Kenny, Fiona Cosgrove, Kieran Roughan, Fiachra Kennedy and Thomas Gleeson; Neil Dargan and Anthony Galvin had previously reconnoitred. Members also paid visits to Ballinakella at other times and in other months; they were always welcome.

Arthur MacAdoo, brother of the then Archbishop of Dublin, whom I had known in Cork, asked earlier in the year if he could bring his scout troop for a camp. I had already accepted that July would be suitable. Our neighbour Christopher Moriarty agreed to lease his house to accommodate the girls. The CYE camp and the arrival of the Scouts overlapped. The two parties got on well although there was, I believe, some removing of tent-pegs and similar innocent fun. One of the highlights was a sailing trip to Killaloe in Brendan Foley's large ocean-going yacht. It was quite a relief when, after an open-air Ecumenical Service conducted by Father Treacy and me, the CYE participants left for their homes; I had no responsibility for the Corkonians.

The following Thursday I drove four CYE representatives to the Ballymascanlan Hotel in County Louth for cross-border talks under the auspices of *Co-Operation North*. We arrived late and went straight to the Conference room; the rest of the delegates were already seated. *Co-Operation North*, the Governments, youth organizations from both sides of the border, and several other bodies were represented to discuss the possibilities of young people from Northern Ireland and the Republic working together towards a better environment. I had suggested many of those participating, such as architect Paddy Shaffrey, David Rowe, Doreen Corcoran and Anne Loane. There were others such as UCD Environmental Studies Professor Frank Convery, and Anton Trant of Trinity College, Dublin. Northern representatives included Ronnie Hill, Headmaster of Enniskillen High School, later to be comatised following the town's devastating War Memorial bomb, and one time Tourist Board Director Maeve Hill of Narrow Water, near Newry. Our own delegates were Kieran Roughan, Jennifer Dinan, P.J. Kenny, Louis Forte and John Kelly; Louis had spent his early years in Belfast, so was a particularly beneficial addition. Our deliberations enabled us to air our thoughts and to get to know each other; we had produced a very professional dossier, *CYE and Our Aims*, which was well illustrated by photographs of members in action. The conference ended at about four in the afternoon, following a general consensus that full support be given to promoting cross-border youth co-operation and exchanges with an environmental basis.

As we had plenty of time and as we were so close to the border with Northern Ireland, I suggested that the young participants may care to visit Newry. Having ascertained that they would all like to make the trip, and that they believed that their parents would not be unduly worried, we said our farewells and got into my Peugeot 305 Estate car. They were naturally quite excited at the prospect of entering the

'North', only Louis and John having previously spent time there. As we climbed the tree-bounded Dublin to Belfast main road through Ravensdale, I told them about the suspicious khaki-clad men I had observed in the adjoining woods some years previously and how the customs posts had been destroyed by bombs. About a kilometre south of the border, we heard a rumble; seconds later, the queue of north-bound traffic came to a halt. A patrol had been ambushed and about thirty cars ahead, a vehicle was smoking as drivers and pedestrians rushed to help the injured.

The scene was not pleasant as we slowly continued our journey, arriving in the town at about 4.45 pm. I was less familiar with the centre of Newry than I am today; each time I had driven to Belfast, I had usually skirted the town on the bypass road to the east. This time I turned into the long straight main street and, seeing an interesting looking store on the right, parked down a street to the left.

As we had only a short time for any shopping, I told everybody to get out of the car and make their way to Bennetts. I then locked the vehicle and followed. Halfway there, I realized that I had left my money behind. Imagine my consternation when, reaching the car, I realized that I had used the automatic locking system and that the key was still in the ignition. I tried every conceivable way to open the hermetically sealed windows and the boot, but the task was impossible. I joined my party and suggested that one of them might like to accompany me to the local Royal Ulster Constabulary barracks.

Within seconds John Kelly and I were tramping the considerable distance to the police headquarters. I explained my predicament, but they were not particularly forthcoming; naturally, they had more important concerns. *"Listen, go back to your car and wait - we'll be along shortly."* We made our way out through the safety of the wire-protected entrance with the uncomfortable feeling that weapons, albeit officially held, were trained on us. At the car, which I had parked outside a publican's premises, I sent John for the others.

After twenty minutes, an armoured vehicle turned into the street. From it disembarked two armed and uniformed constables who took up a defensive stance at one end, and two at the other. Meanwhile the vehicle pulled up beside my Clare-registered Peugeot. More police then searched under and about it, but didn't seem particularly concerned as to how to get the doors open. The sergeant then declared:

16

"I'm sorry, there's nothing we can do. You'll have to call the AA."
They drove off as rapidly as they had arrived.

I managed to get some sterling - I hadn't been prepared for such an adventure - and rang up the Automobile Association. Their nearest patrol was in Belfast, so we would have to wait. As we wandered around, keeping close to the car, Mrs. Madden appeared at the pub door. After having ascertained our problem she invited us in; I decided to remain outside while the others watched television in the bar. A short while later a pint of Guinness was thrust into my hand: *"You must be thirsty now - drink this on the house."*

After an hour, my five young companions got bored with watching television; anyway, they wanted to see what was going on. I posted Daniel and Louis at the entry to the one-way street while the rest of us chatted at the car. A squeal of excitement indicated the arrival of the AA patrol, but it passed the top of the street and stopped behind a Vauxhall Station Wagon of similar size and colour. Before we could reach the scene, the two boys on lookout were astonished as they watched the uniformed patrolman leap out of his van, try the Vauxhall doors and then prepare to force open the window.

"Stop", I cried, *"aren't you the person we sent for to help us get into our Peugot Station wagon?"*

"Aye; isn't this it?"

"No, this is someone else's car; it's a Vauxhall."

As we reached the car, an inquisitive crowd surrounded us. The patrolman, duster in hand to protect the paintwork, reached into his pocket and produced a screwdriver and a bent piece of wire.

"This is how it's done here. We're not unused to this sort of thing..."

I could not help but feel discomfort at the comparative ease the job was done. I had found it impossible to get into my previous Peugeots. This time I had left just enough gap above the window glass to enable an expert to prise the mechanism. With relief, I thanked him before he returned to Belfast. We then rapidly made our way towards the border. I was trepidatious as to what parental reaction there would be following the event, and to the future of the organization. In fact, the relief at seeing their offspring safely home possibly overrode any fears for their safety that their families might have had.

The following week, on the 23rd July, we had another cycle trip. This time we had Alexander and Roxane Rakic from Holland staying; naturally they joined us. It was a roasting day as the party, which included Maeve Ringrose, P. J. Kenny, Kieran Roughan, John Kelly and Elinor Hitching, left Ennis early for Quin Abbey and then on to Tulla. I followed in my car to ensure adequate warning to traffic and in case of accidents; it was a useful excuse for me not to cycle. Anthony Galvin side-tracked by leading a few followers to a nearby cave and it was the beginning of Brendan Ringrose's dedication to cycling. The highlight of the tour was a visit to the Toomeens near Tulla. In several places I showed the participants how the underground river's natural ceiling had fallen in. They were impressed, too, with the natural theatre where the Molonys of Kiltannon once performed plays and gave concerts before their family, staff and tenants. The river was refreshingly cool, so many members splashed their faces, and each other.

When we reached the ruined castle nearby, everybody was itching. Masses of flies had invaded the corpse of a young calf; in their attempt to escape attention, several including Elinor Hitching and Deirdre Kelly ran straight into a patch of nettles. Otherwise, even though they were exhausted, they had had fun. Few members didn't fully enjoy the many activities we undertook each year; some undertakings were quite tough.

On Saturday, the 6th of August 1983, an encouragingly large group turned up to participate in a wheelbarrow push from Shannon to Ennis. Fiona Cosgrove, whose idea it was, designed a thrice folded A4 brochure to be handed out to those who contributed money; it contained information on CYE, YEF *(The Young Environmentalist Federation)* and CFMH, the *Clare Federation for the Mentally Handicapped*, for whose local workshops we were seeking funds. A narrow yellow slip was given to each donor to indicate appreciation for their support. The main object was to clean up the appallingly litter-strewn margins of the busy main road, but we also raised useful money for the handicapped and publicised our organizations.

The group met at the Maid of Erin in Ennis, many dressed in fancy dress. An unsuspecting shopper from Shannon was asked to judge these; Kieran Roughan won first prize. Two of the older members bore a large CYE banner; there was also an assortment of wheelbarrows, some of which bore posters such as *"CYE Litter-gatherers"*. A number of parents joined us in their cars to transport the party to Shannon, several with trailers. The event required a lot of organizing, especially to ensure the safety of those who would be working and walking one of the busiest roads in Ireland. The fancy dress, which many continued to wear, added to the spectacle as some, delegated to thrust empty plastic 'buckets' towards slowed-down motorists, collected money while others filled their barrows. The litter was emptied into the trailers at regular intervals.

Progress was slow and the trailers were already almost full before we reached Clarecastle; there had been a tremendous response. Road-users had heeded our signals to slow when approaching and passing us, safety having been one of my major concerns. It was a particularly enjoyable day and even after fifteen or so kilometres of walking and hard work, there was an air of happy achievement. Ice creams were provided all round.

Shortly after the wheelbarrow push, Anthony Galvin, who had done much of the organizing, presented Senator Tras Honan, Chairperson of the *Clare Federation of the Mentally Handicapped* with a cheque for £150; it was a useful contribution to their funds. Anthony was accompanied by Fiona Cosgrove, then CYE Chairperson, Jennifer Dinan and Maeve Houlihan. Although the same names frequently appear, there were few idlers in CYE; almost everyone pulled their weight.

What was to become an annual trip to Lough Derg on the Shannon also took place in August; there were more clean-ups and cycle trips bringing in Gort in County Galway, Kilbaha, Carrigaholt, Ballyvaughan, and other areas mainly within Clare. Artist and teacher Phil Brennan of Shannon talked on marsh birds and their habitats, and Bill MacInerney of FÁS lectured fascinatingly on the Aran Islands, using his own excellent slides.

Flag days were a useful exercise in perseverance and honesty. At that time there were no problems with either. Young people would be posted at strategic points along the main streets of Ennis, while others would take up positions outside the entrance to Quinnsworth at the Shopping Centre. Others would call to shops where they knew the owners or staff. Beforehand, permission had to be obtained from the local gardai who allocated specific days to specific organizations. Each child had to have a copy of the permit, and a CYE identity card. Most Ennis people, and those visiting for their shopping, were outstandingly generous. Many had read of our activities in the local papers and were in full support. Occasionally there were those who were offensive; perhaps they were taking advantage of their adulthood. Tourists were seldom as forthcoming but occasionally an American would produce a handful of dollars. Our 1983 fund-raising was held on 9th October; funds had almost been exhausted, so the amount collected helped to eliminate our fears that we would be unable to continue.

October's car tour to the wooded Mount Callan Estate on October 15th 1983 was different from the previous two or three events. Leaving the Old Ground Hotel, our regular gathering place, at two o'clock in the afternoon, our party of some thirty participants was greeted by Robert Tottenham outside his front door. As usual, Mike and Marjorie Normile, Dr. Tom Fitzpatrick and his wife, and the Galvins, together with a number of other parents, provided transport. We were given a fascinating guided tour of Robert's forestry and garden in spite of it being a dull and drizzly afternoon.

In November, Derrick and Meg Gordon kindly invited us to visit their goat farm near Inagh, half way between Ennis and Ennistymon, and to learn how St. Tola's cheese is created. Their flock of white goats was most popular, especially with Majella Coll, Orla Staunton and Elinor Hitching. Most of the male members of the party seemed to be more excited with a discarded Fiat 600, which they 'commandeered'. We were concerned that the invasion had exhausted our host and hostess; they still had to continue with milking and their daily routine.

A small number of members descended on Maeve Houlihan's home for the afternoon of Saturday 26th November. It was hoped to produce briquettes from old newspapers. An expensive levered presser had been purchased from England. The papers were soaked in a barrow-full of water before the pulp was moulded into rectangles. The process took a lot of time and was hard work; in the end it was decided that the project was a flop.

During the year, there were two editions of the magazine, which was re-named *Todchai An Chlár*. The spring edition was a professional-looking twelve-page booklet with a cover designed by Fiona Cosgrove. Neil Dargan wrote the editorial while, apart from my *Letter from the Hon. President*, there were articles by Maeve Houlihan, Tina and Gillian Normile, Finbarr Fitzpatrick, S. Warner, Thomas McMahon and others; it was sponsored by Syntex of Clarecastle. Three hundred copies were sold.

The Christmas *Todchai An Chlair*, the Irish of the name being slightly adjusted, was compiled by an editorial committee chaired by Anthony Galvin. Maeve Houlihan, P.J. Kenny, David Kelly, C. O'Donovan, Deirdre O'Callaghan, Fiona Cosgrove and Ray Conway all played their part in producing a much larger and brightly covered thirty-two-page A5 journal. There were lots of fascinating articles by Thomas Gleeson, Deirdre Kelly, Gerry Slevin, Maeve Houlihan, John Galvin, Elinor Hitching, Mary Ruane and Sister Francis; P.J. Kenny contributed pages on astronomy. Each page was sponsored by different supporters of the organization. Thanks were expressed in the editorial to the *Clare Vocational Education Committee* for their £100 contribution to funds, to Sister Francis O'Dwyer and to the Drs. Fitzpatrick, the Normiles, Galvins, Dargans and other parents for assisting with transport to the various events. Others singled out included Mr. Clenaghan of Ballysillan Primary School in Belfast, Mr. Gibson of the Church Hill Centre in County Fermanagh, Dorothy Madden of Ennis, Iseult Murphy of Adare for helping with a tour of Lough Gur, Rector Talbot of Mountshannon, the Old Ground Hotel, Dr. Paddy Doran of Limerick University, who organized a visit to the Hunt Museum, politician Madelaine Taylor-Quin, and to my wife Grania. Most of the printing and layout was done at Ballinakella.

1983 ended with a party at Ballinakella Lodge on 27th December. Most families were otherwise occupied and the long distance meant that not a huge number turned up. It was a pleasant gathering, though, and Grania and I were presented with a cheque by Marjorie Normile on behalf of parents and members. It was a kind and generous gesture, and with the money we purchased a long-desired slide projector. Now we could enjoy viewing our own slides and be able to illustrate CYE talks. There was also a lucky dip, an exchange of gifts and a winter ramble across the fields. The fact that two of the four scholars who scored overall top marks in the Honours English paper of the Leaving Certificate were Raymond Conway and Neil Dargan helped to cap a terrific year. Many activities had been undertaken and CYE membership had rapidly increased.

CYE AILWEE CAVE NATIONAL AWARD BROCHURE

CHAPTER FIVE

1984 followed much the same pattern as the previous year. In January we climbed what the participants named Fountain Mountain, the delightful burren-like area of cragland near Fountain Cross, south of the Ennis to Lahinch road. When we reached the summit of the hill, now being quarried for road surfacing, we discovered an unusual hollow of stones. Was this an ancient monument or possibly just a nineteenth- or early twentieth-century lookout for British troops? Nobody from whom we enquired could give us an answer.

A clean-up of St. Columba's Church of Ireland graveyard, Harmony Row, and Bindon Street in Ennis took place in February. This was later followed by an orienteering session on the sand dunes at Fanore. Organized by David Rowe, it was a great success, though some found it difficult to map-read; a few participants lost their way. The views of Galway Bay and the Aran Islands were spectacular.

We had lots of committee meetings throughout the year, most of which I felt obliged to attend even though I didn't wish to interfere with the running of the organization. There were also further day visits to Ballymascanlan in County Louth over environmental issues in conjunction with *Co-Operation North*. I gave talks on our aims and on the Federation to groups such as Mr. Cunningham's *Salthill Youth Club* outside Galway, the *Newbridge College, Kildare Young Environmentalists* and a group in County Offaly. I had a great deal of correspondence with interested parties throughout Ireland. Although I encouraged CYE officers to write letters of major significance, such as invitations to present the annual awards, I felt it unfair to expect busy students to forgo too much of their free time. In April, for example, I was corresponding with Cardinal Tomás O Fiaich in hopes of his becoming a YEF patron. He had to decline but wished us *"every success and your work should be gratefully appreciated by the adult community - you are certainly training the younger generation to be good citizens."* He signed the hand-written letter himself. Another letter in my possession is particularly touching; it was written by Ronnie Hill, the headmaster of the Enniskillen High School whom I had first met at Ballymascanlan. He referred to group visitations and continued: *"...we intend going ahead with the Co-operation North project."* For a couple of years we worked together; sadly, Ronnie was amongst those at the War Memorial Service in Enniskillen when eleven people were killed by an IRA bomb. He is still in a deep coma.

On the 23rd February, I received a letter from Aras an Uachtaráin. *"The President has asked me to thank [CYE] for the kind invitation to be their Guest of Honour at the 5th Annual General Meeting... and to launch the Young Environmentalist Federation... for Saturday, 21st April provided that he is free from State obligations at that time"*. This was a great boost for CYE and a challenge for its members. We had to submit a programme for Dr Hillery's approval.

At 7.30 p.m. on the day, the choir of Colaiste Muire, thanks to CYE Vice President Sister Francis O'Dwyer, always active behind the scenes and present at most functions, were to sing or play the presidential salute and the National Anthem on His Excellency's arrival. They were to be joined by two boy members. At 7 pm, there would be a Welcome in Irish by Chairperson Fiona Cosgrove, followed by greetings in English by Anthony Galvin, another short speech in Irish by Sister Francis, and I was to deliver an introduction. At 7.30, the President was scheduled to undertake the presentation, each award being preceded by a short biography read by young individuals who would then call their respective awardees to the podium. At 8 pm, a break would signify the bi-partite nature of the evening - the presentation of CYE Awards and the launching of the Young Environmentalist Federation, which we were founding to bring various groups together nationwide - and help participants to enjoy refreshments and to meet the President. After twenty minutes, Dr. Hillery would deliver his speech and launch the Federation, following which he would be the recipient of a small token of our appreciation. The event would be finished at least ten minutes before nine to permit Bishop Harty and his parishioners attend the Easter Vigil in the nearby Roman Catholic Cathedral.

When the day came, there was a great thrill amongst members, parents and helpers. The population of Ennis seemed also to be experiencing the vibes; they were enthusiastically supportive.   I had to be calm and to slow the hypertension without dampening the excitement. The Old Ground Hotel in Ennis would pull out all the stops to welcome Ireland's first citizen.

It was a sunny spring evening outside as I answered a barrage of pertinent questions and tried to oversee the organization of the members, the award recipients and a substantial audience of church, government, county and urban representatives, friends and supporters. Over the noisy chatter in the conference room, once the Ennis town hall, a young committee member breathlessly shouted: *"He's coming"*. I rapidly followed him down the stairs and towards the open main door of the hotel. As we reached it, the fanfare was being played and the doors of the large black presidential saloon being opened. We greeted Dr. Hillery and I introduced him to officers of CYE and the YEF before escorting him to the podium. There was tremendous applause for Clareman Paddy Hillery, who was personally known to many of us; he had only recently been instituted as President.

Everything went according to plan. The *Clare Champion* reported: *"...the large attendance at the launching... was given an insight into the type of initiative fostered by the Young Environmentalists..."* Awardees included Sean O Murchadha, later Vice-President of the *Clare Archaeological and Historical Society*, for his contribution to the development of the County Library, and Chris O'Shea and Lisa Davala, American designers of characterful traditional shop signs, who received the Shield for Design and Architecture. Community Enterprise went to 'Tuath Eochta' of Feakle, Nature to Danny Greene, a CYE supporter who did much to ensure the protection of badgers and wildlife; while the *Clare Environment Council* Shield for Convenience-Food Outlets went to Tulla restauranteur Frank Maheady in recognition of his regular efforts at keeping his village litter-free. Kieran Roughan was chosen for his efforts within CYE, while craftswomen Katherine Cahill and Mary Clair of Ennistymon received the *Industry* Award for their tourist centre.

In his bi-lingual address the President said: *"We all owe an immeasurable debt of gratitude and appreciation to the Clare Young Environmentalists... not only for their work which they have already done with such dedication, but also for making all of us more aware by their example of the threat which hangs over our environment.*

Their loving concern for the well-being of the environment which we all share they have expressed in exemplary action on behalf of all of us. It is an expression of patriotism of the most creative and enduring kind. For that they have earned our gratitude and applause and, more importantly, our full-hearted co-operation, encouragement and support.

The zeal of groups such as Clare Young Environmentalists must inspire us all to play our part in the great task which they have shouldered. The launching of the Young Environmentalist Federation today bears witness to the success of their work. It shows growth and expansion, bright hopes and commitment.

I wish the Federation success a thousandfold. It is a most significant and promising development. Each of us can assist and participate in its crusade by caring for our immediate little corner of the environment. Ní neart go cur le chéile. It gives me very great pleasure to launch the Federation. Guí, gach rath air."

In my words, I emphasised the need for continued support for voluntary work and how one of the problems of present-day life was the squeezing out of the unpaid volunteer in favour of the professional. Our fifth Awards Presentation had been a tremendous success and celebrations continued long after the President's departure.

The following Easter Monday, there was excellent national press coverage of the event. The *Clare Champion* undertook a half page feature, which included a photograph of the Head of State surrounded by recipients brandishing their award-shields. There was also a picture of Regina McDonagh of Barefield.

There were now some three hundred Clare members of the Federation and small branches were being established in other areas throughout the island; similar unaffiliated groups were being formed, too. Our YEF adult *Advisory and Assistance Board* included the then RTE head of publicity Louis McRedmond, Father O'Beirne of Newbridge College, Rita Childers, *An Taisce* council member David Rowe, Maynooth student and first Chairman Neil Dargan, and Sister Francis O'Dwyer. I was kept increasingly busy visiting and talking to schools and youth clubs.

Our 1984 summer camp commenced on the warm and dry second Sunday in July. The twenty-five or so participants included Brendan, Maeve and Orla Ringrose from Kildysart; P.J. Kenny, John and Michelle Kelly, Jennifer and Daniel Dinan, Elinor Hitching, Deirdre and Sarah Kelly, Thomas Gleeson, Louis and Benny Forte, Brian Lynch, Kieran Roughan, Orla Staunton, Fiachra and Breffni Kennedy and Fergus Locke, all of Ennis; Donna Moloney from

Kildysart; Edward Hardy of Banagher, County Offaly; and three from County Kildare. Tents were pitched by most members; P.J. Kenny and Kieran Roughan slept on bunk beds in our store behind the house, surrounded by food. The Fortes had donated pizzas and chips.

The first night, the heavens opened. The four-man nylon tent was blown down, forcing Brian, Brendan and Edward to join those in the store. Our neighbour Christopher Moriarty kindly let us use his recently built bungalow where some of the girls bedded for the rest of the week, and where much of the cooking took place. Grania had the tumble-drier going all day drying bedding, towels and clothes. The participants, however, didn't seem to mind the weather; each morning began with a swim in the lake.

On Tuesday, we went by bus to Bunratty Folk Park via taxidermist Ronnie Morkell's display at Broadford; sadly, he was closed. A visit to St. Mary's Cathedral in Limerick and the recently opened Granary, a restored warehouse, were followed by a conducted tour of the Limerick Civic Museum, and some of the local Georgian streets. Killaloe Cathedral was also viewed. In the evening, I related ghost stories; some members felt a little uncomfortable in the dark silence, in spite of being surrounded by their friends.

The next day, there was a boat trip to Iniscealtra where we visited the round tower and ruined churches. One of the late Liam de Poer's archaeologists showed us their sites. A minibus journey to South Galway and North Clare on Friday took us to the Devil's Punchbowl at Gort, Coole Park and Thoor Ballylea, and to Dunguaire Castle at Kinvara from whence we travelled to Ballyvaughan and experienced Ailwee Cave. Grania and Sister Francis awaited our return till nine pm.

Following a water fight, and fancy dress competition on Saturday, everyone helped to prepare for visitors. The girls produced food while the boys laid out seating for the ecumenical service. This was conducted on the lawn by Whitegate native Father Treacy, Dean at the Diocesan College in Ennis, until he left the post in 1997, and me; the first hymn, as before, was "*Shall we gather at the River?*" After lunch, there was peace following the participants' departure. Grania and I relaxed with our feet up.

The following month the Doctors Fitzpatrick, Mrs. Ringrose and I drove Finbarr Fitzpatrick, Thomas Gleeson, John and Michelle Kelly, Daniel Dinan, Kieran Roughan, Tara and Cathy Mooney,

Regina O'Dea, Niamh Long, the three Ringroses, Stephen Rynne, P.J. Kenny, Elinor Hitching and Jennifer Dinan to Counties Fermanagh and Donegal. En route, I offered to show my carload Monsignor Horan's new runway at Knock. There was nothing to prevent us from driving onto the newly-surfaced strip, so I raced down it as though to take off. Suddenly, I realized that, being on a mountain-top, we were about to be propelled into space. Luckily my brakes were good. Another carload went by Tuam and stopped at Drumcliff in County Sligo where they saw W.B. Yeats' grave. On arrival at Cloughglass near Burtonport, we camped on the sand dunes by kind permission of Warren and Anne Loane. The weather was perfect and most members swam in the Atlantic.

Killybegs, its harbour and fishing boats were visited the following day. A quick lunch in Donegal town was followed by a tour of the Castle. We then crossed the border at Belleek before continuing to the Lakelands Leisure Centre at Enniskillen. Bellies full of sweets and coke, then cheaper in the North, we pitched our tents at Monea Castle, thanks to Dr. and the late Mrs. Dick Brandon, and rapidly went to sleep. Some were a little nervous at having seen several military patrols. The Saturday saw us driving through Enniskillen, where some swam at the Forum, and on to Armagh Planetarium; astronomer P.J. Kenny was particularly delighted. We saw over the Church of Ireland and Roman Catholic Cathedrals and walked about the town. On return to Monea, the members held a disco until well into the night. After breakfast on Sunday morning, tents were folded and loaded before we drove to Enniskillen. Most went to Mass in the Roman Catholic Church while I made my own way to nearby Rossorry for a Church of Ireland Service. It was a successful visit and we shared activities with local schoolchildren.

The major August event was a camping trip to the Clab valley in the Burren and to O'Dea's nearby goat and cheese farm. Regina O'Dea, who was a member of CYE, showed us a cave and other interesting sites on her family property. A three-man film crew camped with us and we were videoed at Eagle Rock, St Colman MacDuach's cave, Michael Cusack's house, the wedge tomb at Commons Hill, the Burren Perfumery, where the then owner Brian Mooney gave us a long interview, and at various other sites. On the Sunday, following Mass in Carron Church, we had a re-run of Brian's interview. Tara Mooney was particularly popular with the boys. After lunch we continued filming at St Fiachtna's Penitational Stations and at Corcomruadh Abbey before swimming at Bishops Quarter. The three Kennedys, whose parents kindly brought their camper, Orla and Brian Cosgrove, John Kelly and Fergus Locke, John Fitzsimons, Kieran Roughan and Anthony Galvin were joined by Gaël du Jonchay, a French boy who was staying with us. Matt Purcell and other associates of CYE were involved in a very professional first-run.

At the end of October, a large number of members spent the holiday weekend at the Cusack Centre, a youth hostel and facility in the north of the Burren run by the *Clare Vocational Education Committee*. Kate Purcell played her guitar beside the huge fireplace, while the younger boys and girls sang Irish and popular songs. Committee member Niamh Long of Tuamgraney helped with the supervision; Mrs. Ringrose and Mrs. Kennedy, both parents, were also active and assisted in the daytime. It was necessary to ensure no broken limbs while participants traversed jagged rocks and some very rough terrain.

The first day, a walk up the west face of Turlough Hill to the early Iron Age hill fort, and then down the steep north slope to the early Christian churches at Oughtmama, exhausted everybody. Few had been to this unspoilt area, so it was particularly exciting. At night, everybody slept in communal dormitory bunks; silence reigned before long, except for the loud snores indicative of deep sleep. The next tour was to the west of the centre when we scrambled through Scailp na Seisrí, a deep cleft in the mountainside reputedly created during the eighteenth-century Lisbon-centered earthquake, which devastated many of the area's castles.

The November event was a tour to Killone Abbey near Ennis, along the ancient pilgrim road. The scramble through briars and scrub was an adventure; some of the party got lost. Also in November, we undertook a clean-up of White Strand on the Atlantic Coast, but it was cold; the work only lasted for about an hour, even though car-boots of rubbish were returned to Ennis.

In December, Donal McHugh, chief executive of the *Institute of Industrial Research and Standards* at Shannon, kindly showed us the work they were undertaking to eliminate pollution, and other projects of the government-sponsored unit. CYE members, observing

29

through a special glass aquarium, were fascinated by the reaction of salmon or trout in flowing water, when pollution was introduced. The tour had been initiated by our friend Rick Bolens, a senior member of the staff. We were also invited into the Control Tower at Shannon Airport to see how incoming, outgoing and overflying aircraft were carefully guided. Aeroflot allowed us to climb aboard a Russian aircraft, and we had a general tour of the airport thanks to Aer Rianta and Shannonside directors, for whom I was then working. There were, of course, further activities at Christmas.

CLARE: PAST, PRESENT & FUTURE 1989

CHAPTER SIX

The event of the year for 1985 took a tremendous amount of organizing. Our visit to Mallorca was stimulated by personal experience; Grania and I adore the island and its people, especially Grania's cousin Jacqueline and her Mallorquin husband Pepé. Whilst visiting the previous year, I had learnt of a threat to an offshore island, Dragonera, where speculators were seeking permission to build holiday developments.

On Good Friday, twenty of us (CYE members and three or four others) left Limerick by coach for London where we were booked into an inexpensive hotel. On arrival, we were horror-struck: the rooms were dirty, the sheets unchanged and there were used male protectors and human excrement in the bath. Furiously I reprimanded the front desk, but only a nightwatchman was on duty. Many of the room doors of this unstarred West-End hotel were unlockable. As there were questionable strangers around, most members of the group doubled up so that there were several in each room. Even so, I spent a sleepless night; a number of youngsters knocked on my door because they were suspicious or nervous.

With relief to know that on our return we would not be staying in the same place, we swilled down our soggy toast and marmalade with weak tea, and met up with Sister Francis who had been staying in outer London with members of her family. Her nephew David O'Dwyer kindly gave us a tour of Westminster Cathedral and the nearby Abbey, the Army & Navy stores and several sights. We left Gatwick Airport for Palma on a chartered Boeing 757, having journeyed to it by monorail. Following the three and a half hour flight over France and Spain, we were met by Jacqueline Catalá and a fleet of cars driven by generous volunteers including Jeremy Gullyford whose wife comes from Dublin. They convoyed us to Jacqueline's conveniently-situated house above Port de Andratx. We were accommodated in her upper floor apartment for a pittance; she had kindly accepted my request that we base ourselves there. The girls had one room under the supervision of Sister Francis and I kept an eye on the boys' dormitory. It was an ideal set-up as the apartment also had a substantial reception area and a well-equipped kitchen. A separate outside stairs led from a large balcony outside the kitchen to the garden in which grew fig trees, orange trees and attractive local flowers; in front, overlooking the Port of Andratx and the wide mountain-bordered valley, was a swimming pool. The town was a short walk away. Jacqueline and Pepé treated us as members of their family. Even when the upstairs lavatory got blocked through overuse, Jacqueline personally undertook the unpleasant task of clearing it. She also helped the Palma airport authorities to locate a purse and other items stolen from baggage, presumably at London Airport.

The day after our arrival was Easter Sunday, and it was important that we receive Holy Communion especially on this day. As three or four of us were members of the Church of Ireland and there is no Episcopal Church of Spain in Mallorca, I asked the local Roman Catholic Priest, with whom I was acquainted, if we could have permission to share the Eucharist in his church. This is something we could not do in Ireland due to Roman Catholic Church rules. The Episcopal authority speedily gave us full authority to receive in the local church, and within their jurisdiction, whenever we needed. It was a heartfelt and much appreciated display of Christianity which did much to promote ecumenism; the move was appreciated by us all.

In the morning we practised the Spanish, Catalan and Irish hymns we would sing for the evening Mass, while that afternoon was spent climbing the nearby Atalya, a steep craggy mountain where at the summit, I showed the climbers the remains of what I believed to be a promontory fort; I had come across it a couple of years previously. It was a tough climb for young people who were not used to long-haul travel or the balmy heat. The view from the top of the mountain, one side of which is a cliff, is spectacular but I was terrified lest one of the party should slip over the edge.

At eight in the evening, the *Clare Young Environmentalists* lead the singing of the Irish Hymn *"Be Thou My Vision"* at the special Easter Mass. Our shared participation of the Eucharist was a moving experience. Afterwards there was a warm welcome from the community, many of whom I knew or had met previously.

On Easter Monday, an exciting but daunting drive took us on the twisty and somewhat dangerous road along the mountainous west-coast of the Island to the tenth-century farm known as La Granja, the Grange. Many of the party surreptitiously imbibed of the Sangria, a refreshing mildly alcoholic traditional Spanish wine and fruit drink, provided free from a 'self-service' barrel; a couple of the boys became particularly talkative. La Granja is fascinating for those who are interested in antique farm machinery and such unusual indoor items as olive presses and wine barrels, all in their original, often rather dusty state. There are watercourses and a mill too, and native Mallorquin poultry, dogs and pigs; the smells are evocative. We continued to Santa Magdalina, a hilltop monastery which thrusts itself from a nearby area of the central plain, before showing them old Palma including the magnificent cathedral with its vast and colourful medieval rose window.

The following day, after a long night's sleep, we went to the Delphinarium. I had arranged that Brendan O'Regan and Ciara Long be invited to ride in a small boat hauled by two of the dolphins; they got great applause. The zoo, the aquarium, the miniature motor bikes, remote controlled boats and the airfilled bouncing castle were so popular that I couldn't collect the scattered participants at closing time. As the place was wel policed, it was a relief not to worry too much about supervision. There are some delightful photographs of Timothy Hyde, James Thorrington and Laurence O'Loughlin doing the rounds of the noisy motorbike course.

Wednesday saw us walking the quiet country roads to Andratx, the main town of the valley; plain and almost featureless but somehow characterful houses line the narrow squared-off streets. There we visited the old market and mixed with the stallholders, North African and native, and haggled over bargains. To some the chickens and other livestock, and the garden produce were the most interesting; others enjoyed the unusual nick-nacks and local souvenirs.

Lunch was provided by our American friend, Nancy Surmain, in her typical Mallorquin *casita*. She showed us the tiny interior and explained how she cooked in the local way. Afterwards, nearly everyone sat in the sun. Nancy showed us two small caves before we ambled home. Some, such as Sarah Kelly and Derek O'Connor, were exhausted; they were the youngest and not used to walking long distances. That evening a disco was arranged in the Catalá's roadside garage beneath the swimming pool patio. Their Spanish friends and son José, now a married fishing-boat owner with a young daughter, joined the fun, but there was a language barrier.

On 11th Aprdratx school-master Don Juan gathered some of his Secondary School pupils to meet us at nine in the morning. The car drivers, with me in the lead, conveyed natives and visitors to the start of an exciting walk beyond the small seaside resort of San Telmo. We clambered along plant-bordered mountain paths and up immense limestone crags; unique vegetation was pointed out and we were told about the local fauna. The views were breathtaking from high above the calm sun-soused Mediterranean; eventually we reached an old abandoned Trappist Monastery surrounded by finely constructed terraces and walls. A popular Irish activity at the time was breakdancing; ice was broken as CYE members instructed the local youngsters. Traditional Irish songs were exchanged with those of Mallorca and Catalonia. After a swim from the beach at San Telmo, we sailed home by ferry.

That evening, a special reception took place on the Catalá's swimming pool patio; the Mayor of Andratx was presented with a letter of greeting from *Clare County Council* Chairman, Johnny Moloney. Specially designed parchments were presented to other dig-nitaries and various helpers; I conveyed a message of thanks and hopes for further links, especially as Spain was then about to join the Euro-pean Community. The Mayor and other speakers, including the Secretary of the Local Government and representatives of local schools and clergy, reciprocated. The *Clare Young Environmentalists* behaved impeccably, passing round food and drink and practicing their broken Spanish; Sister Francis, aided by Lawrence's mother Sheila O'Loughlin, ensured that eats were mainly reserved for guests. Some, however, such as Thomas Gleeson and Kieran Roughan, were caught on camera surreptitiously devouring tit-bits on the perifery.

Friday morning was spent visiting the Mediterranean fish labo-ratories located on the opposite side of the harbour. The scientific breeding of species unknown in Irish waters was particularly interest-ing, and the microscopes popular.

The final and significant event of our tour to Mallorca was a visit to the five-kilometre-long Dragonera Island, which lies parallel to the Southern tip of the Western mountains. We had to obtain special permission, which, in spite of our objections against development, was obtained from the owners. We hired a special passenger boat for the afternoon and made our way out of Port de Andratx and under the impressive russet-coloured cliffs at Mallorca's South-West tip before crossing the wide stretch of water which divided the island from the mainland. The predominant island wildlife seemed to be the ferral pigs who fed on the lizards, *dragones*, which give the island its name. There was also an elderly ass. Shortly after landing on the little pier, we climbed a steep path to a clearing in the scrub where we enjoyed a picnic lunch sitting on an ancient winnowing pad. As we commenced our meal, one of the inquisitive pigs snatched Sister Francis's worldly goods; only after an exhausting chase was her handbag recovered. The old watchtower was an attraction and several went for a stroll up a narrow laneway towards the Island's summit; I warned them not to climb too high for I knew that there is a sheer drop on the western side. Here was perfect peace, similarly unspoilt by modern man.

By the end of our visit everyone expressed their enjoyment. There were tears as farewells were exchanged. Friendships had been created and hopes expressed that there would be an exchange visit by the Mallorquin children. Later, Don Juan had to tell me that, because so many were from poor families, few could afford the necessary expenditure. Tomás Porcell who is a native of Port de Andratx did, however, organize the twinning of the Scariff and district Chamber of Commerce with the Port de Andratx Council. Unfortunately, this relationship has lapsed.

At London's Gatwick Airport, Sister Francis collected the only baggage trolley available to convey our assortment of suitcases, boxes, ensaimadas and other purchases to the appropriate railway platform. As we made our way with the heavy load, it was obvious that one of the axels of the trolley was bent. Like a limping man, one wheel rose and fell to a rhythm. Sister Francis and I were in stitches of laughter, which infected the others and onlookers. We almost missed the train.

Early the following morning, having boarded the return coach to Limerick, I gave the go-ahead to the driver; having roughly counted our passengers, I had assumed that all were aboard. He started the motor. Suddenly, round the corner appeared P.J. Kenny, struggling with a heavy suitcase. Everything had gone so smoothly until then that I had allowed my sense of responsibility to lapse. It was with relief that a further recount indicated *all present*.

In a letter for the Most Reverend Teodora Ubedo Gramage, Archbishop of Palma, our patron Bishop Michael Harty had sent greetings from Killaloe diocese and had commended us. He ended his letter: "*In this international Year of Youth, these young Irish people wish to share their yearning for peace and justice with the young people of Spain...*" These sentiments had been shared by us all.

The Mallorcan visit put the rest of the year's activities in the shade. There were lots of clean-ups, local excursions and committee meetings, many taking place at Maeve Houlihan's home on the Gort road, or at Kieran Roughan's following his election to the Chair. The editorial committee for the re-named *Clare - Past, Present and Future* would now represent *Clare Youth Impact*; some of the committee members believed the new nomenclature would improve our image.

In June, a busload of Enniskillen High School pupils stayed at the Hydro Hotel in Lisdoonvarna. P.J. Kenny, John O'Halloran, Brian Costain, Thomas Gleeson, Brendan Ringrose and I shared two days of activity; we camped on a field belonging to MaryAngela Keane outside the town. One evening, after a trip to Ailwee Cave and the Cliffs of Moher, the two parties joined for a disco at the Hydro. The din still rings through my head as I recall the brightly flickering lights and gyrating youth, with whom I found myself forced to strenuously participate. The following day we visited Shannon Airport; the party was somewhat subdued following the 'night before'.

Later in the month, there was another Burren visit. Thomas Gleeson, Orla Staunton, Brian Costain, John O'Halloran, Brendan Ringrose, Benny Forte and Daniel Dinan were amongst those I joined for a short camp beside the turlough below Mullaghmore, near Tubber. There was barely enough soil to peg the tents. Amongst the activities was a long trek across the Burren, following a 'green road' towards Carron and crossing the high Commons on the track which leads down to the then half-built thatched cottage constructed of local stone by the Dutch Bartelink family. They had few public facilities such as mains electricity but their fairy-tale house and its cosy situation caused wonderment amongst the participants who left with purchases of Edam and Gouda cheeses. There were complaints on the return journey as we traversed difficult terrain, the loose sheets of stone on the uneven rock base causing many to lose their balance.

The 1985 summer camp was attended by some of those who had been with us in Mallorca; about twenty-five, an easily manageable number, participated. They included Orla and Brendan Ringrose, Donna Molony (all from Kildysart), Thomas Gleeson, Daniel Dinan, Carole and Thomas Neylon, Benny Forte, Amanda Hamilton, Tim Hyde (Aughrim), Gerald Geary, Kevin O'Gorman (Dublin), John and Michelle Kelly, Ciara Long, Edward Hardy (Banagher), Brendan Clune (Tulla), the two Logan boys from Clarecastle, Gäel du Jonchay who was staying with us from France, Kieran Roughan, Deirdre Kelly, Brendan and Denis O'Regan; Sister Francis assisted.

Kevin's father Fergus O'Gorman, then involved in environmental affairs nationally, gave an interesting lecture; our neighbour Allie Kay set up her loom and demonstrated weaving, and Vivienne Foley, an internationally known local ceramicist, showed us how to create porcelain. There was also a visit to Coole Park, Lady Gregory's demesne near Gort, where we met Professor Etienne Rynne (a friend and supporter) and his son Stephen. There were also trips by boat to Holy Island and by foot to the Dane's Den, a small cave in the Slieve Aughty Mountains behind Ballinakella.

One mid-day, I was called to the telephone. As I was supervising the cooking of potentially dangerous hot soup and vegetables, I didn't feel justified in leaving the young chefs on their own. I hadn't realized, though, that the caller had already talked with Grania. I was delighted to learn that I had won a holiday in Portugal. This had been common knowledge to all but me, and there were cheers as I made my way back to the campsite kitchen.

A minibus excursion was undertaken to the Rock of Cashel, where some of the boys enjoyed rolling down the grassy slopes. Another day we went to the ruined Cullane House near Kilkishen, in government care under the Forest and Wildlife Service. Though I told them the early history of the house and showed them the gardens, the campers had more fun clambering up a vast multi-branched cedar.

Our next journey was to County Fermanagh. A dozen of us, including new members Turlough Mooney and Pat Connole of Carran, camped in a field immediately adjoining the Loanes' house near Ballinamallard. Apparently the main tent was destroyed by the 'unhinged' adult leader, which resulted in the occupants and other members spending their last night on the floor of a farm building. We visited the Marble Arch Caves, the Lakeland Forum and Enniskillen Castle, Castletown (where we were kindly welcomed by Dr. Dick Brandon) and Monea Castle. We also drove to the Lough Navar look-out above Lough Erne and had a boat-trip to Devenish Island where participants visited the monastic remains. On the Saturday, some members found themselves inadvertently participating in an Apprentice Boys' parade.

A treasure hunt in August saw frantic participants speeding through country roads between Tulla and Ennis. Also, during the same month, several members camped at Ballinakella Lodge where amongst the games enjoyed was 'strip spin the bottle'; each bout was terminated before the penalties accrued resulted in any 'full montys'. There was also a visit to Scariff Show. In December there was the usual Christmas party.

CLARE: PAST, PRESENT & FUTURE 1987

CHAPTER SEVEN

In January 1986 there was a walkabout in Clarecastle with participants collecting rubbish and tidying up the area, mainly around Clare Abbey; it was a rather haphazard exercise.

The Annual General Meeting in March took place earlier than usual, and in early May, we had another *Co-Operation North*-sponsored week-end with a busload of participants from Irvinestown. We toured the Shannon area and south-east Clare on the first day, whereas on the Saturday we went to Fanore and the west of the Burren.

The Awards Presentations took place later in the month at the de Valera Library in Ennis; joint guests of honour were *Clare County Council* Chairman Sean Keating, a resident of the Loop Head Peninsula, and *Ennis Urban District Council* Chairman Paddy Coote. Amongst those who received recognition were the *Cloughleigh Residents Association*, introduced by Mark Kearney, and Ireland's first woman steeplejack, Mrs. Angela Collins O'Mahony for her encouragement of meaningful pursuits at the recently developed Landscape House recreation centre. Both Elinor and her mother Maura Hitching accepted different awards while Paddy O'Sullivan, an expert on pine martens, was given the Shield for Nature.

The March activity was a visit to Ailwee Cave where those who came were generously welcomed by Roger and Susan Johnson; they and those involved in their projects have been most generous to CYE. At Easter, a bus was hired for a trip to Killarney where we stayed at the Mucross Hostel, which was once a Church of Ireland place of worship. Many local places of interest were visited and the keepers of the national park took us on patrol in their jeeps at night-time where we observed deer and other nocturnal creatures.

The summer camp involved the usual events, it being a particularly sunny week. Justo Romero from Spain, popular with the girls, was staying with us. There were boat trips to Iniscealtra, island on Lough Derg, and a couple of night patrols. There was one long-distance journey when we hired a coach to Aughnanure Castle near Oughterard in County Galway and then spent time in Galway city visiting St. Nicholas's Collegiate church, Lynches Castle and the Spanish Arch.

The rest of the year there were trips to Dysert O'Dea Castle and Archeology Trail, the Burren Wildlife Symposium and the Claureen and Drumcliffe area near Ennis. There was also a talk on ceramics by Vivienne Foley, and a generously supported clean-up of the Cois na h'Abhna Music Centre grounds at Ennis, as well as the usual discussions and editorial plannings.

Designated their Year of the Environment by the European Community, 1987 saw a number of incentives restored or undertaken following the February CYE Annual General Meeting. On St. Patrick's Day, members manned a stand at St. Flannan's College during the Clare Youth Club day. I encouraged several members to enter the Gaisce Presidental Youth Awards; sadly none completed the difficult tasks they set for themselves.

The organization's Patrons, the two Bishops of Killaloe, jointly presented the Environmental Awards in May, this time at the West County Hotel. By now there were eight categories. Martin Browne authoritatively chaired the event. Diarmaid Ó Donnabháin, Principal of the Shannon Comprehensive School was congratulated for organizing his school's Environmental Day; National Teacher Lucy Hastings-McGrath from Newmarket on Fergus - always an active supporter of CYE - shared the Giving of Themselves Award, and John McNamara and David Hely-Hutchinson, introduced by Yvonne Howe, got the *Clare Champion* Wildlife Shield. Other awardees included author Sean Kierse of Killaloe, Father Harry Bohan, and Father Eugene Nugent who accepted the Tom Mannion Shield on behalf of the *Ennis Co-operative Enterprises Society*. Martin Browne was himself selected as the person who had done the most to promote *Clare Youth Impact* during the year. Councillor Anne Arthur-O'Brien of Ennis and other speakers praised mambers for their efforts. At the end of the evening, the chairman, as the Ennis-based *County Express* reported, *"produced a few rabbits from up his sleeve"*. Sister Francis, Grania and I were presented with specially commissioned plaques on behalf of the members, now numbering up to four hundred; our efforts were thankfully recorded. We were touched by their thoughtfulness and impressed by their ability to keep their task a secret.

Tom Coffey gave us another of his tours of the Inchicronan area later in April and showed us some unusual pre-historic and later monuments. The following month there was another clean-up of the Maid of Erin.

The July summer camp, when we had Gilles Missud and Claude Fraysse from France staying at Ballinakella, and other events were as usual well attended, and there were trips to the Fota Wildlife Park, where we enjoyed the many wild animals and the 'train ride', and Blarney Castle in County Cork, where there was a queue to kiss the Stone. We also hired a bus to Kerry and visited Muckross House and the Torc Waterfall where Tomas Gleeson swam fully clothed in the rocky stream. It was quite hot. A mountain hike to the Dane's Den in the Slieve Aughty Mountains meant trudging across sphagnum moss and over a quaking bog. There was also a visit to Portumna Wildlife Park where participants climbed a watchtower to observe birds and where they also saw deer and other animals. The Reverend Patrick Towers, now Rector of Nenagh, gave an excellent sermon at the end of camp, during which he symbolised the way we treat the earth by throwing a globe at his son Alex as though it were a football.

1987's major project was the launch by County Council Chairman Pat McMahon of *Clare - Past, Present and Future* on 20th September. Edited by Martin Browne, it was the most professional magazine so far. Well sponsored by *Ennis Urban District Council*, the *Clare Vocational Education Council* and commercial enterprises such as *Guinness Peat Aviation*, *Essco Collins*, the *Ennis Bookshop*, *Syntex* and the *Electricity Supply Board*, it had articles by *Radio II*'s Billy Browne, Tom Coffey, *Radio Telefis Eireann* personality Don Conroy, author Gordon D'Arcy, historian Gerry O'Connell and P.J. O'Sullivan whose Bats and Pine Martin pieces were particularly apt; Eamon de Butlear wrote on Irish rivers. Members produced some excellent reading; Sister Francis contributed two articles, and David MacCarthy had a delightful poem on the town of Ennis. Michelle Arthur also wrote on the old church at Newmarket-on-Fergus, Carole Neylon on Killarney and Aidan Coll on Ennis Abbey. Graveyards in my Parish was the subject chosen by Newmarket's Rose Slattery, Bunratty Castle by Niamh Flynn and the Ralahine Co-Op by Maura O'Loughlin. Sinead Ryan had an article about the Great Clare Gold Find of 1854, and there were also excellent pieces by Joseph Molony and Martin himself. Sean Spellissy and John O'Brien compiled a riveting quiz, which was illustrated with a number of photographs. The magazine

41

was a most worthy contribution to the reading available during the year.

The following Thursday, I accompanied editor Martin Browne, Maria Cotter, Louise Roberts, Aidan Coll and Kieran Roughan to Aras an Uachteran where a copy was received by President Hillery. Dr. Hillery was full of praise for all that CYI was doing, and generously provided refreshments; he also gave us a conducted tour of the residence. His warm person-to-person conversations with the young members was touching and the resulting photographs and publicity enhanced the organization's future.

It was now increasingly difficult for me to continue undertaking my many commitments. These included the *Clare Environmental Council*, founded the previous year, and the *East Clare Clean Environment Group*, which had been founded by Anne Moloney of East Clare to rid Lough Derg of pollution. I was rotating Chair of the former and Chairman of the latter, a task which I accepted for a maximum period of one year.

The *Clare Environment Council* was founded to unite the county's voluntary and professional groups to share and attempt to solve local problems. In the Ennis Library earlier in the year, I had convened a gathering of some twenty-five invited participants; Sonia Schorman of the *Shannon Archaeological and Historical Society* recorded the minutes. Various Tidy Towns groups including Ennis and Tulla, Angling Associations, the *Society for the Protection of Animals*, the *Burren Display Centre* and the teaching profession were present. Minnie Baker represented the *Clare Tourist Council*, but the only two from State or Semi-State bodies were Martin Bradley of *Shannonside Tourism* and Anne Arthur O'Brien, an active member of *Ennis Urban District Council. Clare Youth Impact* was to the fore. The council was abandoned after a year or two due to a lack of active support, but it achieved a good deal.

To get *Clare Youth Impact* insured as a youth club for a reasonable premium we joined the *Clare Youth Council*, affiliated to the *National Union of Students of Ireland.* They were most helpful and we made use of their Ennis headquarters, but we were a different kind of club to the parochially based groups and had a different outlook, ethos and aims. Due to an open-house policy, we began to attract young people who were not as dedicated to the environment as previous members. Some parents were using us as a crêche while they played golf; some new members were calling for more entertainment such as discos. Although CYI was, to all intents and purposes, being run by its increasing number of members, I had to step in and back the committee to keep the group on its environmental course. Perhaps our theory that these young people were the ones we should be encouraging was misguided. Did they really want to understand what the world is about and promote environmental issues, or did they merely wish to cash in on us as a well-organized club with a small annual subscription?

At this time, an increased public awareness was encouraging politicians and businesses to become involved. The *Department of Education* introduced more environmental issues into its curriculae and such companies as *General Motors* backed environmental competitions with huge prizes; compared to these, the pittances we offered for our recipients was chicken-feed. Our efforts were being capped by the multi-nationals; our County Clare schools' poster competition was an embarrasment. Even the Chairman of the *Clare County Council* introduced his own generous environmental award, although it seemed to be aimed at professionals. *Clare Youth Impact* backed voluntary effort and had played no small rôle in inceased environmental awareness. I did realize, however, that in a few years time, as when the churches' social responsibility had been purloined, government enthusiasm might wane; that could trigger a revival of such groups as *Clare Youth Impact*. Whatever the case, we would continue with our efforts while at all feasible.

CHAPTER EIGHT

Our activities for 1988 started in February with a party in the Youth Centre; it wasn't terribly successful and, although requested by the general membership, was poorly attended. Father Gerry Kenny kindly supplied music. A walkabout in the Cragleigh and Drumcliffe area the following month saw a better turnout and some litter was collected.

Tomás Porcell from Mallorca was now staying at Ballinakella and was able to assist in the organization of the awards presentation in April. Cathaoirleach of *Seanad Eireann* Treas Honan, who was Guest of Honour, emphasized the need of financial support for art, design and theatre in order to create job opportunities for young people. The event in the West County Inn was well attended and amongst those present was Minister for the Marine, Brendan Daly, who had presented the previous year's awards; Deputies Síle de Valera and Donal Carey were also there. The Senator said that *Clare Youth Impact* was an example of young people playing their part in today's Clare and today's Ireland, and that criticism from 'Hurlers on the ditch' should be ignored. Sister Francis, Martin Browne, Grania and I were singled out for our exceptional work. The Senator suggested that CYI might consider taking on the task of monitoring any legislation relating to environmental issues as it progressed through the houses of the Oireachtas. She outlined the Air Pollution Bill of 1987 as an example, and suggested that we could discuss with, and have some qualified person to talk to, Parliament about it. These were encouraging and far-sighted words. I referred to the positive rôle of adults who supported the organization, and Sister Francis emphasized the need to beautify the country to encourage tourism.

David McCarthy, who had now become chairman, indicated that the awards reminded him of John F. Kennedy's famous quotation *"Ask not what your country can do for you, but what you can do for your country"* and Franciscan Guardian Fr. Rory Aherne told us that as St. Francis was the Patron Saint of ecology, members of his Third Order would like to become more involved.

For the awards, Aidan Coll was considered the member who had done most to promote CYI; he had worked tirelessly behind the scenes. Sonia Schorman, editor of *The Other Clare*, received the McKenzies of Cork Shield for History; Fr. Sean Sexton, the Maurer's of Ennis award for Education; wheelchair-confined Tony Melican of Newmarket-on-Fergus was recognized with the West County Shield for his Tidy Towns and fund-raising activities, and the Convenience-Food Shield went to Vincent Keenan for his thoughtfully designed 'Chicken Empire' in Ennis, and for his ensuring that the surrounds were litter free. Ornithologist Jacinta Reynolds got the Wildlife Award and the *Garda Siochana*, who were represented by Aidan's father Sergeant Coll, were given recognition for the design of the new Clare Divisional Headquarters in Ennis. Their awareness of the past and their pride in the present ensured that the Sparlings of Scariff Shield for Community Effort went to Maeve Smyth and the Ennis Arts Festival, while Sean O Domhnallain of Ennistymon got the Industry Award for restoration on his business premises. The event was successful, thanks to the work of the long-standing and mature Committee.

A group from Enniskillen and Irvinestown under John Walsh, assisted by Mary Kerrigan and John Fielding, joined us for their May visit. A tour of Shannon Airport, Craggaunowen, Bunratty and Mooghaun was organized. As they came mid-week, only a few of our members shared the event. They were an interested and delightful group.

Eight West Clare students swept the boards in our Environmental Art Competition late in the year. Sandra Collins of Bealaha, Jacqueline Kelly and Nicola di Lucia of Kilkee, Claire Clancy of Lisdeen and Angela Behan of Doonbeg were placed first in their categories while Miriam Roche, Anne Carroll and Patricia Blake were runners up. Nicola was adjudged overall winner.

Presenting the prizes, I particularly congratulated Kilkee Convent Secondary School and encouraged the pupils towards greater environmental participation.

The weather for the 1988 summer camp was appalling. Each of the five girls and ten boys paid £42, which included the cost of food, excursions, overall insurance at £103, and general expenses. The ridge pole of our Icelander tent snapped in a gale the first night and it rained for the remainder of the week. Three older members, and a French visitor, camped separately at the top of the field. Gort and Galway were again visited. We made a major excursion to Dublin to see the Wax Museum, the Zoo, where koala bears were the main attraction, and the magnificently restored ESB Exhibition house in Merrion Square, which had been the British Embassy until it was destroyed by a terrorist bomb. Because of the rain, we had a second excursion, this time to the Devil's Punchbowl near Gort where participants were shown how the river disappears underground before exiting at a nearby cave. We had a picnic lunch at Coole Park and visited Aughnanure Castle near Pughterard. The return journey took us to Maam Cross and along the north coast of Galway Bay, with a stop at Loughrea for refreshments. Allie Kay demonstrated weaving another day, and Christopher Moriarty talked about eels. The £38 collection at the ecumenical service before dispersal was given to *ClareCare*.

In October our funds were boosted by the generosity of the *Brother Corporation* who allocated us £250 from their sponsorship fund. Our friend Ron Graham, now a Church of Ireland auxiliary priest, was then Director and fully supported our efforts.

As Tomás Porcell, now involved with helping CYI, is Spanish and as Ireland was celebrating the anniversary of the Spanish Armada, it was decided to perform a pageant. I produced a chronological course of eight historic scenes with narrations. An introduction read in English, Irish and Spanish, outlined Ireland's links with Spain from the time of Milesius to the European Union in poetic prose. In the first scene, David McCarthy as Milesius declared himself; Jack McMahon was his general. The three queens, Éire, Banbha and Fodhla were acted by Louise Roberts, Sharon Malone and Maria Cotter, respectively. Tomás Porcell acted the part of Philip II of Spain and Mairead Doyle, Queen Elizabeth of England. I can't recall why Carol Neylon acted as Archbishop MacCann, or Niamh Carmody as the Spanish bishop; perhaps we had run out of boys. More than twenty-seven members took part. The small audience in the hall at St. Flannan's College was thrilled. Unfortunately, there were too many other activities on the Thursday before Christmas and a larger crowd attended the dress rehearsal than the final event. It was a disappointment for those who put so much into it, but they enjoyed displaying their acting talent.

The second volume of *Clare - Past, Present and Future* was also published at Christmas. Martin Browne, assisted by Aidan Coll, was responsible for the editing and Tomás Porcell, the designing. The organization was now calling itself *Clare Youth Impact - the Clare Young Environmentalists*; the name was soon to revert to its original. The logo on the cover, however, was still CYI.

In this magazine there was the inducement of two plane tickets to Dublin for the winner of Martin's Megaquiz, sponsored by *Aer Lingus*. *Poparama*'s Billy Brown contributed a delightful illustrated piece on Exploring the Shore, Deirdre Corry four pages on Craggaunowen and Auriol Considine an illustrated article on acids. Gordon d'Arcy wrote about a slow worm population on the Burren, Lorna Guinnane about whales, and Don Conroy compiled two instructive articles, one on drawing people and the other titled The Artist in You. Sean Spellissy's Boethius MacClancy and the Spaniards was illustrated by an amusing photograph of the author in the uniform of the 'Spanish Order of the Ocean Sea', an honour which he had been awarded earlier in the year. Poems included an evocatively written *Ode - Written at Dusk near Doolin* by Anthony Galvin and an anonymous selection in *Poet's Corner*. The publication lived up to the reputation of its predecessors.

In May 1989, *Clare Youth Impact* and the *Clare Environment Council* jointly shared one of the inaugural Clare Community Awards sponsored by the *Clare Champion*, and the Cork and Limerick Savings Bank (now the Trustee Savings Bank). It was a welcome stimulant. A photograph in the *Clare Champion* depicted Sister Francis and me holding a cheque between us. On one side of us was Flan Galvin whose three sons, Anthony, John and David, were members of CYE, and on the other, bank director Michael Conlon. The back row consisted of Aileen Byrne, David McCarthy, Martin Browne, Martin Coffey of the bank's Ennis branch, Lucy Hastings-McGrath, and a smiling Aidan Coll, recently appointed CYE Chairman.

Headmaster of Scariff Community College, John Kelly, was congratulated at the CYE Annual Awards presentation; he had just published his book on the Bodyke evictions. Another East Clare recipient was Anne Moloney, founder of the East Clare Clean Environment Group. Tom Coffey's efforts at recording the county's history were rewarded, and Mr. and Mrs. Enzo D'Auria, David McCarthy, Anthony Galvin, Padraig Quinn and Risteard Crimmins got awards in other specified fields. Morgan Llewelyn, glamorous authoress of *The Lion of Ireland* and other best-selling books, was Guest of Honour. Fr. Rory Aherne, O.F.M., County Council Chairman Michael Guilfoyle, Sister Francis and I were also included in the official photograph, published in the *Clare Champion.* A new metal logo was displayed.

There was no magazine and, as I only returned from a three-week drive to Turkey on 7th July, no summer camp; the previous year's members had mainly been new to the organization and I felt that without adult help, which I had tried to solicit, the task would have been too much for us. A few senior members such as Brendan Ringrose pitched their tents in our field at our invitation. We did, however, foster a wild Burren goat under John MacNamara's scheme to save the endangered species. The animals were being devastated by unscrupulous poachers who were selling them in England to satisfy Arab demand.

We had enthusiastic offers to participate in the Flag Day from a lot of recently enrolled members. Flag days, which took place at the end of August, became somewhat disastrous. In 1989, I had been late for a preliminary meeting held in Colaiste Muire when a glass-windowed door was broken. Nobody owned up to it, something which had never happened before. At the meeting, however, I felt that I couldn't discriminate as to who would collect; those who wished to do so were given sealed plastic boxes. Several seals seemed to have been tampered with as senior members of CYE counted the collections; the amount collected was not reflected in the returns. The Committee and long-standing members were horrified; it was a psychological blow. A sinister element had begun to infiltrate our organization.

Although we had the odd party, treasure hunt or other kind of meeting, I found the almost 100-kilometre journey to Ennis and back, and the devotion of so much time, increasingly arduous. The organization had a fantastic and dedicated membership, but my health and a lack of active general support exacerbated my lack of dedication in the future. I persisted, however, and still devoted weekends to CYE, mainly for the sake of loyal and dedicated long-term members and some very keen now blood; they were still refreshingly supportive.

CHAPTER NINE

The spring awards presentation for 1990 took place in Cois na hAbhna, the magnificent modern Ceoltas concert centre, the grounds of which we had tidied. In May, our friend Minnie Baker helped arrange the venue and organize refreshments. Guest of Honour was Minister for State Brendan Daly, T.D., who used the event to declare 20,000 hectares of the Burren a National Park. Opposed to unsuitable development in areas of special scientific interest, he supported the opposition of the *Wildlife Service* to the siting of an airstrip in Roundstone bog for Clifden; he also paid tribute to CYE.

A new award for the National Environmentalist of the year, donated by Ailwee Cave, consisted of a large bronze *Reinhart* owl, a small owl plaque as a keepsake and a substantial cheque, which was to be spent personally by the recipient. The first awardee was Dr. Emer Colleran, national president of *An Taisce*. I knew Emer when I was Chairman of the *East Clare Clean Environment Group*; she was a dedicated and hardworking Galway University marine biology professor who gave freely of her time. In her speech she indicated the dramatic increase in environmental awareness in Ireland. Three years previously, a European Community survey showed the country to have the lowest level of environmental concern among member states; now, during Ireland's Presidency, An Taoiseach had given top priority to environmental issues. In complimenting CYE for initiating the award, Emer quoted a recent speech by Britain's Prime Minister Margaret Thatcher: *"No generation has a freehold on this planet - all we have is life tenancy, with a full repairing lease"*. A photograph appeared in the *Clare Champion* of Brendan Daly, Emer Colleran, directors of Ailwee Micheál Mulqueeney and Roger Johnson, and me with the award.

Others were recongized too; Grania, whom Gerry O'Connell later congratulated in a delightful letter, received an award for her efforts and general support; Carol Neylon took the shield for the most active CYE member, and Frank O'Dea, editor of the *Clare Champion*, was recognized for his encouragement of environmental contributions to the paper. Other recipients of awards included Martin Breen (History), Franko Bonito (Convenience Foods), Susan Doherty, Brendan Kelly of Quinnsworth, Collette Redington and Nuala Mulqueeney.

The other main event of 1990 was Tomás Porcell's editorship of a new *Clare - Past, Present and Future: Hello Clare*. This was a significant achievement for someone who had little English when he joined the organization. He was assisted by an editorial committee of Gerard Daly, Carole Neylon, Sarah Kelly, Eric Flynn, Mairead Doyle, Lisa Gardiner and Barry Molony. Carole and Mairead now shared the CYE chairmanship, Sarah was the secretary and Lisa the treasurer. Although there were slightly fewer contributions than in the two preceding volumes, the standard was still high. Eric Flynn's article on Safe Sunbathing was useful; Paddy O'Sullivan sent another fascinating article on bats and Lucy McGrath wrote A Ramble in Thomond. Poland was the subject of an interview with Mairead Doyle and Lisa Gardiner, while Allie Kay wrote on the inspiration behind her textiles. Aisling O'Leary gave a haunting account of cosmetics and tests on animals and Martin Browne added to his previous literary contributions with his article Stephen Joseph Meany, Journalist, Poet and Felon. There were further articles by Brian Lough, Sean Geason, Patricia Keogh, Grania Weir and David Rowe whose delightful cartoons *Ennis Celebrates* occupied the central page. The Editor and committee received great praise; Martin Browne, who had set the tone in the previous two editions, wrote Tomás a generous congratulatory letter.

In 1991, I found myself at pre-selected venues when only one or two enthusiasts turned up. Most of the more dedicated members had gone on to third level education. The environment was being promoted in schools by the *Department of Education*, and free-time involvement was no longer as welcome. Occasional meetings took place but we began to wind down. I insisted, though, in deference to the sponsors, that the annual awards would continue.

At the end of January 1991, I received a letter from Joseph Brennan, Deputy Secretary to President Mary Robinson. She regretted that due to pressure of existing commitments, she was unable to accept our invitation to be Guest of Honour. She did, however, send her very best wishes for the success of the occasion. An invitation to Minister for Environmental Protection Mary Harney, T.D., whom I knew when she actively supported the *East Clare Clean Environment Group*, was accepted at the end of February.

The Presentation ceremony took place at Ailwee Cave by invitation of the sponsors of our national award. Mary Harney re-iterated the new level of awareness of the environment "*compared to years back*"; this had been achieved through an education process to which CYE had made a major contribution. Referring to the proposal for a national park and interpretive centre at Mullaghmore, then looming as a major issue, Minister Harney said she would listen "*to what people had to say on the subject and try to resolve any points of conflict*".

I stressed that there are always major environmental issues to be tackled and individuals and groups must be prepared to stand up and fight: "*Too much is going on for us to stand idly by. I understand that there is still intimidation of those who protest at what they believe to be detrimental to Ireland's environment. What a cowardly expression of greed in our democratic Christian society... Every citizen of every locality should have a major imput as to what happens to their area. They live there... Although times change and expert advice and assis-tance is necessary and should be heeded, they - of all people - should know how to treat the area which has been their responsibility for generations*". I pointed out that millions were being spent by Europe but "*Is it not bad, in fact dangerous, management that is neglecting the infrastructure of poverty-stricken western areas of Europe... Bad roads mean unfair disadvantages... The young are forced to emigrate; the old can't cope and the whole area suffers.... The environment suffers.*" How true these words have proved.

David Rowe, to become Chairman of *An Taisce*, was presented with the *CYE-Ailwee Cave National Award*. He was then chairing An Taisce's planning division and was their Honorary Secretary. David was getting recognition for his relentless work both on a national and local County Clare basis. Ballyea National School received the Sparling's of Scariff Community Award for litter and rubbish collecting; Anne Keane accepted it. Mary Angela Keane of Lisdoonvarna was presented with the *Clare Champion* Wildlife Shield for the preservation and understanding of the Burren flora; generous draughtswoman and artist Hilary Gilmore took the Old Ground Hotel-sponsored Art, Architec-ture and Design Award, and Frank Kenny the West County Shield for Giving of Themselves, for his rôle in the restoration and maintenance of St. Joseph's shrine - a task shared by CYE. The founder of the Rural

51

Re-Settlement Programme, Jim Connolly of Kilbaha, was given the Tom Mannion Travel Industry Award. Joe Noonan, whose comprehensive and delightful books record the history and folklore of East Clare, received the McKenzies of Cork History Shield, while that for education went to *Clare FM*, the local ratio station who "*are never afraid to highlight major or even minor issues in a fair and responsible manner*". Mairead Doyle was also recognised for her efforts in CYE. Afterwards, the Johnsons provided refreshments in the Cave's restaurant.

Miniature dolmens were the year's keepsakes; active organizers included Harry Hitching, Aisling O'Leary, Carole Neylon, Margaret Downes, Gerard Daly and Sarah Kelly.

As we were winding down our activities, I suggested to the *Vocational Education Committee* that their 1991 grant go towards the annual awards expenses; senior staff officer Stephen Flaherty indicated that they had graciously agreed.

Later in the year, I was presented with the prestigious Iarnród Éireann Oidhreacht award, sponsored in conjunction with the Radio Telefis Eireann radio environment programme. This was partly in recognition of my involvement with CYE. Grania and I had a delightful day's outing in Dublin organized by the railway company.

Mountshannon, where in CYE's early days we held an environmental exhibit backing their *Tidy Towns* win, was two hundred and fifty years old in 1992. The Annual Awards would be presented by Síle de Valera in the parish hall. The May sun shone as the doors were opened and the crowd filed in. Additional attractions were Kate Purcell, who had played her guitar during a Burren visit, and refreshments provided by Noel Lyons and the *Mountshannon 250* committee.

Tim Robinson, who had produced detailed maps of the Burren, the Aran Islands and Connemara, was the recipient of the National Award. Shields were presented to Gordon D'Arcy, still working for youth and writing books on birds; the Newmarket-on-Fergus community, whose trophy was collected by Pat Halpin and Una McMahon for their efforts to keep their village clean and tidy; the Killaloe Village complex; Frank Maheady of Tulla, and John Hunt, who got the Tom Mannion Industry Award for his encouragement of visitors through his hard work, devotion and generosity, especially concerning

Craggaunowen. Although he was in Rome at the time, Father Ignatius Murphy was congratulated for his tremendous contribution to history, especially with the publication of volume one of his comprehensive *History of the Diocese of Killaloe*. Sadly, he died before he was able to complete the final volume, which has been taken on by CYE member Martin Browne. Father Desmond Hillary, recipient of the *Education* award, was cycling in the Burren with a group of his pupils; his involvement in the planting of trees was specifically recognised. Also unable to be present was CYE Honorary Secretary Tomás Porcell who had encouraged the continuation of the annual ceremony; Grania accepted the Syntex Shield on his behalf. Mountshannon Community Council Chairperson Patricia Donnellan accepted the Sparlings of Scariff Award on behalf of the village; their efforts for the year had been tremendous. Local youth, John Cleary, got a special Young Historian Award.

Mairead Doyle opened the evening's proceedings. Other speakers included Sister Francis, Tom Mannion, Pat Donnellan, who is now with the Leader and Rural Development programmes, dedicated County Councellor Paddy Bugler, David Rowe of *An Taisce* and, of course, Síle de Valera, who gave us an encouraging boost. Citations were read by local children including Siobhán Donnellan, Elaine Perril, Deirdre Sampson, Cait Malone, Joseph Dillon, Majella Cahill, Ross Glennon, Carmel Duffy and Sandra Hayes; they were great, and were sincerely thanked. Several longstanding members of CYE came, including Ray Conway, Kieran Roughan and Brendan Ringrose.

I recalled that in countries such as Brazil, developers are prepared to murder to obtain their objectives; those who speak out often endanger themselves and their families. I also expressed our congratulations to County Council Chairman Michael Hillery for initiating his environmental award, its first recipient being Deputy County Manager Riobard O'Cealleagh.

Shortly after the event, I received a touching letter from Father Ignatius (Iggy) Murphy: "*...I am really delighted with the beautifully inscribed 'plate'. It is something I will always treasure. Many thanks also for the gift of 'Illuminations'* (a book of cartoons by Martyn Turner on Irish historical events) - *I had seen it in the bookshops. Very appropriate for a historian to have to dip into now and again. I have the plaque installed - the first time I ever had anything of its* *type...*". In his letter of thanks, Tim Robinson wrote: "*I was delighted, in receiving the trophy from the hands of the Four Provinces in person* (we had four children dressed for each area of the country to hand over the owl), *to note that they are still so young and full of the future. Perhaps in talking about the need for conservation we sometimes over-emphasise the great age of our heritage when the fact to be remembered is that these things, both natural and cultural, are we hope destined for an endless future, and so are in their extreme youth today...*" Síle wrote how much she had enjoyed the evening. It was also delightful to get a letter from Roger Johnson of Ailwee: "*We did enjoy the awards presentation last Friday, the setting in the hall at Mountshannon, the glorious evening, pleasant company and your unique performance all contributed to a memorable and happy event...*"

NOTHING LIKE GOOD SUSTENANCE FOR ALL!

54

CHAPTER TEN

Kevin Joyce, who runs one of Connemara's finest craft shops and a marble factory, sold us ten marble 'books' as the keepsakes for the 1993 award ceremonies. I wrote to Manuel di Lucia who was involved in promoting Kilkee; as the previous annual events had taken place in north, east and central Clare, could the next be in the south west? Manuel was most helpful, as were Eugene O'Kelly, Sister Echaria Ryan and Mary O'Connell, Mr. May of the local national school and our own Sister Francis O'Dwyer.

The Kilrush and District Lions Club generously took care of the expenses at Kilkee's Victoria Hotel, including generous refreshments. Following Eugene's welcome, I mentioned how some of our 'graduates' may eventually find time and enthusiasm to get the organization swinging again. I welcomed John Hunt, recipient of the 1992 Industry Award, indicating how his and his sister's continuance of their parents' foundations at Craggaunowen and the Hunt Museum was appreciated. As Guest of Honour, John presented the awards. Most went to local people such as Sean Cunningham of Killimer who got the Wildlife Award for his agricultural zoo. Matty Shannon and the *Doolin Marine and Rescue Service* were recognized for the life-saving of animals and birds as well as humans, and the Education Award went to Sister Mary O'Connell for promoting awareness amongst her pupils and for collecting material for recycling. The *Kilkee Tidy Towns Project* got the Community Award and Ryan's Café was recognised for its efforts at cleaning up its surrounds. Riobard O'Cealleagh's urban renewal programme in Ennis ensured that he was presented with the Art and Architecture Shield and Michael Guerin of *Aer Rianta* got the Industry Award. A local youth, conspicuous for his efforts in keeping his town clean and tidy, was given the CYE Syntex Award for Active Environmental Promotion. Tom Coffey, historian and authority on Fullachta Fiadhs, was also on the list. The National Award, however, went to the President of Limerick University, Dr. Ed. Walsh, for *"his tremendous leadership in promoting an environmentally beneficial ambiance... through the arts and general education"*

By the end of 1993, I realized that no longer could I almost single-handedly continue to steer the Annual Awards, even though Sister Francis and a few others were generous with their help. The now ten-year-old *Clare Young Environmentalists* had been an extremely active and successful organization.

In January 1994, I advertised an open meeting in St. Anthony's Hall, Ennis. I hoped a member or friend would share or take on the responsibility of CYE; Donal Fitzpatrick, recently returned to Ennis with his children, had expressed an interest, but the task would have been daunting. He was at the meeting, along with Roger and Susan Johnson, Micheál Mulqueeney of Ailwee Cave, Josephine and Nuala Mulqueeney, Aidan and Majella Coll and Tomás Porcell.

I had already forewarned that unless there were adults prepared to steer the organization into the future, I would seek a voluntary group to take over the presenting of the annual awards. I invited several, but the only one represented was *An Taisce*; Michael Roberts had been Chairman of their Ennis branch and was active in environmental affairs.

It was a short meeting. I asked if any of those present would consider taking CYE on; the silence was predicable. Most, out of kindness or loyalty, had come to support a reasonably satisfactory outcome. I then asked Michael Roberts if *An Taisce* was interested. He indicated that, although they wouldn't undertake other responsibilities, they would organize the awards. Some time later, Michael visited us and collected relevant information; he also fetched the owl, which had been delivered to us by Dr. Walsh.

During 1995, I attended five or six special *An Taisce* meetings in the Old Ground Hotel chaired by Annie Wyse of Shannon, Honorary Secretary of the Clare branch. I had promised to assist A*n Taisce* with their first presentation. Usually there were three or four of us; I successfully requested that CYE member P.J. Kenny, living in Ennis but working in Shannon, be co-opted onto their sub-committee. P.J. did a lot, and worked hard at organizing help from the local Shannon schools and locating awardees.

The 1995 event took place on 7th December in the O'Regan room at Shannon Airport. This was appropriate as our Guest of Honour was founder of the *Shannon Free Airport Development Company*, Dr.

Brendan O'Regan, after whom it was named. We pulled a fast one on him as, when he had presented the shields, we announced that he himself would be the recipient of the National Award. Amongst the other guests were *Aer Rianta*'s Harry Galvin and David Rowe, then President of *An Taisce*, who drove down from Dublin for the occasion. Terry Murray of *Murray Associated Architects* received the Art and Architecture Award; Paudie Cosgrove got the Wildlife Award; Gerry McNamara of the Old Cod in Scariff was given the Convenience Food Outlet Shield, and Edward Jamieson of Mountshannon, the Young Person's Award. Other recipients were Graham Meakins of *Tellabs* and Phillip Brennan of St. Conaire's National School, both at Shannon, together with Sonia Schorman, Patricia McCarthy, and Father Albert McDonnell who had been responsible for great improvements to Sixmilebridge. Thanks to Clare *An Taisce*, it was a pleasant evening and participants enjoyed themselves. Local Shannon children read the citations beautifully.

At Christmas 1996, Brendan Ringrose organized a reunion of members, friends and parents in the Old Ground Hotel in Ennis. Grania and I, Brendan and Rita O'Regan, and Roger and Susan Johnson were present as were such parents as Dr. Fitzpatrick, the Kennedys, Ringroses, Hitchings and other long-term supporters. Martin Browne and Brendan spoke, touchingly recalling their happy days with the organization. It was an enjoyable and evocative event and sparked further attempts by some members to work together and perpetuate some of CYE.

Previously, Tomás Porcell, Carol Neylon and members had kindly presented me with an inscribed gold watch. Such acts of kindness have always been appreciated. The re-union was special in that the participants were now adults and seemed to have been remarkably successful.

There was no presentation of awards in 1996 or since. Brendan Ringrose especially, David MacCarthy, Carole Neylon, Martin Browne, Elinor Hitching and Mairead Doyle, who had all held positions of leadership, were amongst those who felt that, because they had benefited from and enjoyed the camaraderie of the *Clare Young*

Environmentalists in their younger days, they would attempt to reactivate some aspects of the organization.

A student of law in Dublin, Brendan asked me if he could observe, as a guest, the Church of Ireland General Synod. Previously we had discussed the possibility of resuscitating the outdoor ecumenical services, which took place at the end of each summer camp. Archbishop of Armagh, Robin Eames, was asked if he would like to address such a congregation. He had already indicated that he would like a quiet private visit and, I having introduced Brendan to him, expressed delight at the prospect. Sadly our own bishop had already booked him for two major events and felt it would be too much to ask him to a third. Supporters of all denominations had expressed interest and would have joined us.

Already a lot of people were involved before we learnt that the Archbishop wouldn't be with us. We then had to decide on a new speaker. The Rector of Drumcree, the Reverend Mr. Pickering was approached due to the controversy over his church being used as an Orange rallying point. Unfortunately he couldn't come in August, which was now the only month left to us due to the progress of time. Eventually, thanks to help from the Reverend Trevor Sullivan of Aughrim and others, we were blessed with two speakers. The Reverend Bob Cobain was a onetime editor of the *Presbyterian Herald* and now ministering in Galway, and Mrs. Claire O'Mahony from Castleconnell, a leading ecumenist involved in organizing the annual Benedictine Conference at Glenstall. The theme chosen was 'Overcoming our divisions on this Island' which was very much in keeping with the ethos of CYE; we were always trying to break down political, religious and other barriers.

Come the first of September it poured with rain; it had been sunny the previous day and the second was terrific. Luckily, Dean Nicholas Cummins had given us permission to use Mountshannon Church of Ireland church should such a situation arise. No way could we have assembled on the lawn. Although only about 130 people came, the event was a success. Introducing it, I outlined the need to consider settled persons versus travellers, refugees versus natives, Catholics versus Protestants, professionals versus amateurs, nationalists versus unionists, and other of division. "*We have to live with divisions rather than eliminate them; strive to overcome them*". I emphasized the need for co-operation and understanding of each other's methods of approaching the same goals. *"Environmentalists unite on common ground..."*

Mrs. O'Mahony indicated that a 'passion' for praying together leads to dialogue and faith in the future: *"we need public witness and to show concern for all"*, she said. Mr. Cobain told participants how the environment is both joy and sorrow: *"we have twisted the world by grabbing... Religion is too often wrapped up in the Union Jack or Tricolour"*. Several people contributed from the audience including Dr. Brendan O'Regan of *Co-Operation North*, Minister Síle de Valera and one time member of the European Parliament, T.J. Maher, who had driven over from Tipperary; Bishop of Killaloe Willie Walsh bemoaned the churches' slowness to see the environmental problem, and Elizabeth Holden, an active Killaloe parishioner, expressed pertinent observations. Louis and Maeve McRedmond, members of the Ringrose family, and film-maker Josephine Glin were amongst those who drove down from Dublin.

Brendan Ringrose had to remain in Dublin to sit exams. Martin Browne, a dedicated organizer, filled the breach. He and Father Brendan Quinlivan rigged up speakers, which had been kindly lent by Kate Purcell's brother Matt. Harry Hitching, another CYE member, played the organ. Afterwards a scrumptious tea was presented, almost totally organized by Mountshannon's Majella Cahill. Lots of participants provided sandwiches and cakes. Everybody chatted vociferously in spite of smaller numbers than had been anticipated.

I do not know what plans Brendan and his committee have for the future. He or any others who wish to attempt to perpetuate the aims and efforts of CYE can be assured of Grania's and my fullest co-operation and encouragement. As a voluntary civic group, the *Clare Young Environmentalists* depends on the goodwill of its membership and voluntary assistance from individuals and from organizations such as *Co-Operation North, Cois na hAbhna*, Ailwee Cave and local community groups. The only financial support from the state has been through the *Clare Vocational Educational Committee*. CYE is, as a member has put it, *"a coalition of interests: young and old, parents and children, Catholic and Protestant (and others), ecumenism, history and ornithology, nationalist and unionist, voluntary workers and business people, which gave it a uniquely wide view of life. This*

59

contrasts markedly with say students unions in universities who have an exclusive radical agenda, an unbalanced one. As young people, I really think it was important for us to have contact with older people from whom we learnt, rather than older people simply being figures of authority". I have hopes for the future of the organization and for its revival to again play an active role in environmental concern and action by young people.

The *Clare Young Environmentalists* have made their mark on Irish environmental awareness. It is a worthwhile project and few participants have failed to benefit from its activities. The public, too, have gained an understanding of what can be done by a small band of dedicated young people. It can continue to be a major influence on the future of Ireland's environment. It is hoped that the awards will soon again be presented. The sparks engendered in past members are still glowing brightly.

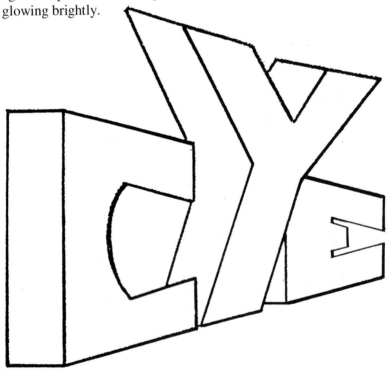

THE CYE LOGO - DESIGNED BY TOMÁS J. PORCELL

PATRONS OF CYE

The Bishops of Killaloe

GUESTS OF HONOUR FOR THE CYE AWARDS PRESENTATIONS

Tadgh MacConmara
Chairman (1982), Clare County Council

Mrs Rita Childers
Widow of President Erskine Childers

Madelaine Taylor Quin, T.D.

Johnny Molony
Chairman, Clare County Council

Bishops of Killaloe
Most Rev. Dr. Michael Harty
Right Rev. Edward Darling

Senator Treas Honan

Author Morgan Llewellyn

Brendan Daly, T.D.
Minister for the Marine

Síle de Valera, T.D.
Minister for the Arts, Culture, the Gaeltacht and the Islands

Emer Colleran
University College Galway, and An Taisce

Mary Harney, T.D.
Minister for the Environment

61

John Hunt
Cragaunowen and the Hunt Museum

Dr. Brendan O'Regan
Founder, Shannon Free Airport, Co-Operation North, etc.

CHAIRMANSHIP OF CYE

Neil Dargan
Fiona Cosgrove
Ray Conway
Anthony Galvin
Maeve Houlihan
Kieran Roughan
Martin Browne
David MacCarthy
Aidan Coll
Mairead Doyle

CYE - AILWEE CAVE NATIONAL AWARD RECIPIENTS

Emer Colleran
University College Galway; An Taisce

David Rowe
An Taisce

Tim Robinson
Cartographer, author

Dr. Ed. Walsh
President Limerick University

Dr. Brendan O'Regan
Co-Operation North, Obair etc.

DRUMCLIFFE
CLEAN-UP
1981

FERMANAGH TOUR 1981

FERMANAGH TOUR 1981
Warren Loane, Finbarr Fitzpatrick, Kieran Roughan, Dr. Fitzpatrick, David Galvin

EARLY DAYS

'IS THAT WHERE THEY WERE THROWN?'

Sister Francis and friends, Roscommon Castle

'PILGRIMS' ON THE ROAD TO KILLONE ABBEY

SPANISH POINT LITTER CAMPAIGN   KILDARE Y.E., 1982

ST. TOLA'S CROSS, DYSERT O'DEA, OCTOBER 1982

THE NORMILE BOAT, BALLINAKELLA, FALL 1982

AWARDS PRESENTATION 1983 (Photo Shannon Development)

Ray Conway, Dean Maurice Talbot, Mrs. Rita Childers and Hugh Weir

CRAGGAUNOWAN, SEPTEMBER 1983

KILTANNON 1983

'TRY THATAWAY'. ORIENTEERING, FANORE SPRING 1984

OUT OF THE MOUTH OF THE CAVE, GORT

ROCK OF CASHEL 1985

MOUNT CALLAN FOREST WALK

DANCING AT PORT DE ANDRATX, 1985

MALLORCA 1985

Timothy Hyde, Deirdre Kelly, Kieran Roughan, Jennifer Dinan and friends

MALLORCA
P.J. Kenny, Derek O'Connor, Sarah Kelly, Ciara Long, Tim Hyde,
Thomas Gleeson, Jennifer Dinan, Deirdre Kelly

A DRAGONERA BACKDROP FOR A HIBERNO-HISPANIC GROUP 1985

GOING FOR A JAUNT, KILLARNEY 1986

TORC WATERFALL, KILLARNEY 1986

A LARK IN THE RIVER

TORC, KILLARNEY 1986

ST JOSEPH'S WELL CLEAN-UP, SEPTEMBER 1986

HEAVEN NEXT STOP? (CULLANE)

INISCEALTRA ROUND TOWER, SUMMER CAMP 1987

SUMMER CAMP GROUP 1986

ARAS AN UACHTERÁN: President Hillery receives Magazine copy. 1987

SMILE PLEASE! R.T.E. Video 'I live here', CO. FERMANAGH, JULY 1989

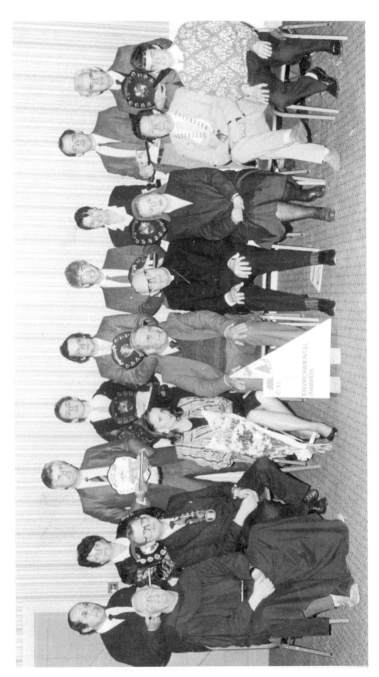

C.Y.E. AWARDS PRESENTATION, ENNIS 1989 (*Photo The Clare Champion*)

AILWEE CAVE, 1991 AWARDS PRESENTATION
Lucy Hastings McGrath, Minister Mary Harney, Hugh and Grania Weir

Roger and Susan Johnson, Tomás Porcell and Mairead Doyle

Tomás Porcell and his "HELLO CLARE" Editorial Committee 1991